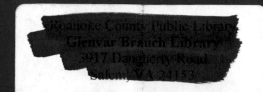

D1486937

FOR MICHAEL
WHO IS 25

[redacted]

AND FOR
UNCLE RALPH
&
DEE-DEE

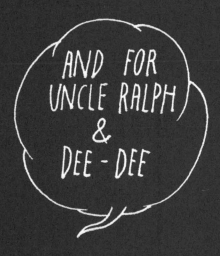

FANTAGRAPHICS BOOKS 7563 Lake City Way NE | Seattle, Washington 98115

Edited by Gary Groth | Designed by Leah Hayes & Adam Grano

Promotion by Eric Reynolds | Published by Gary Groth and Kim Thompson

| To receive a free full-color catalog of comics, graphic novels, prose novels, and other fine works of artistry, call 1-800-657-1100, or visit www.fantagraphics.com. You may order books at our web site or by phone.

Distributed in the U.S. by W.W. Norton and Company, Inc. (212-354-500) | Distributed in Canada by Raincoast Books (800-663-5714) | Distributed in the United Kingdom by Turnaround Distribution (108-829-3009)

ISBN: 978-1-56097-888-6 | First Fantagraphics printing: March, 2008 | Printed in Singapore

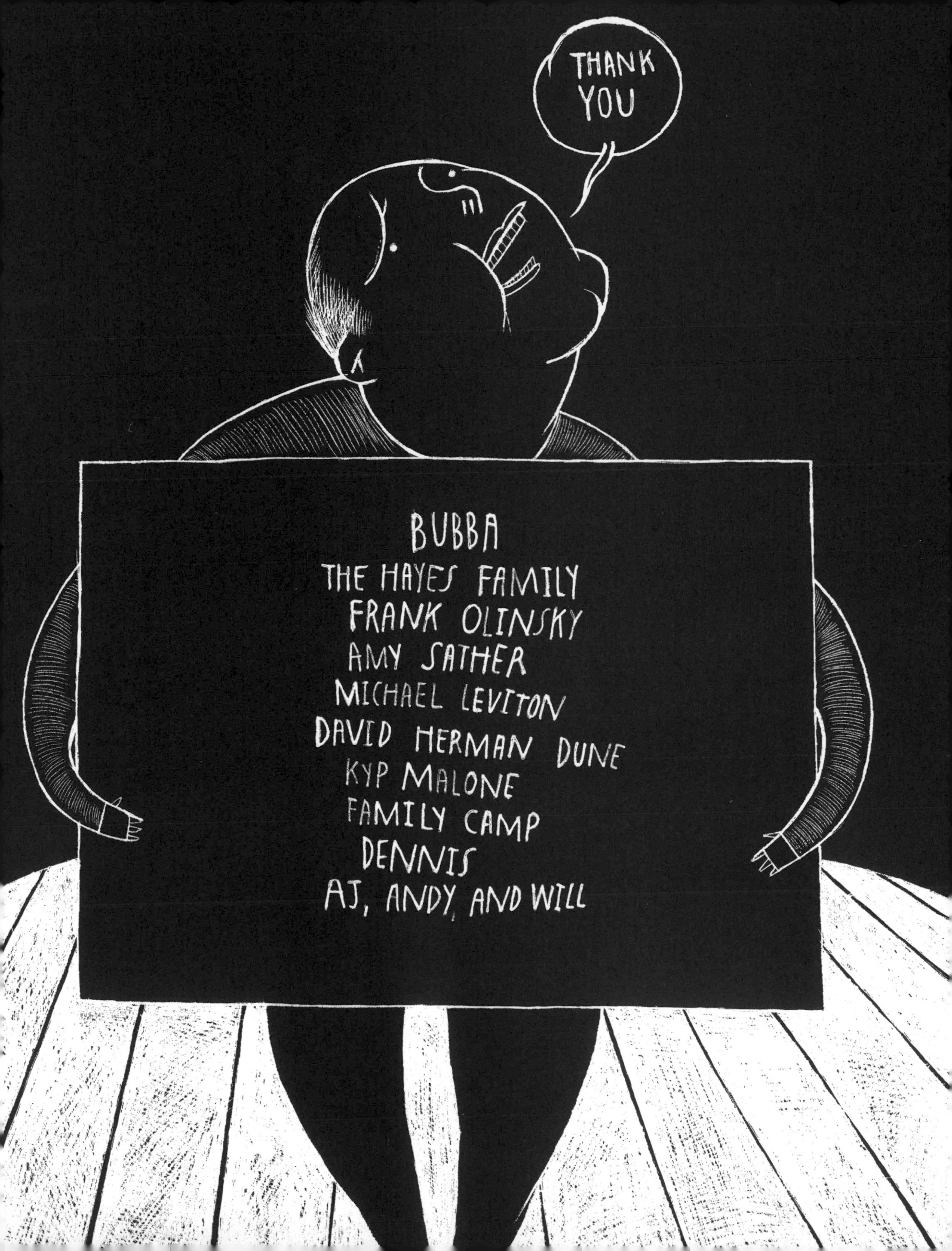
THANK YOU
BUBBA
THE HAYES FAMILY
FRANK OLINSKY
AMY SATHER
MICHAEL LEVITON
DAVID HERMAN DUNE
KYP MALONE
FAMILY CAMP
DENNIS
AJ, ANDY, AND WILL

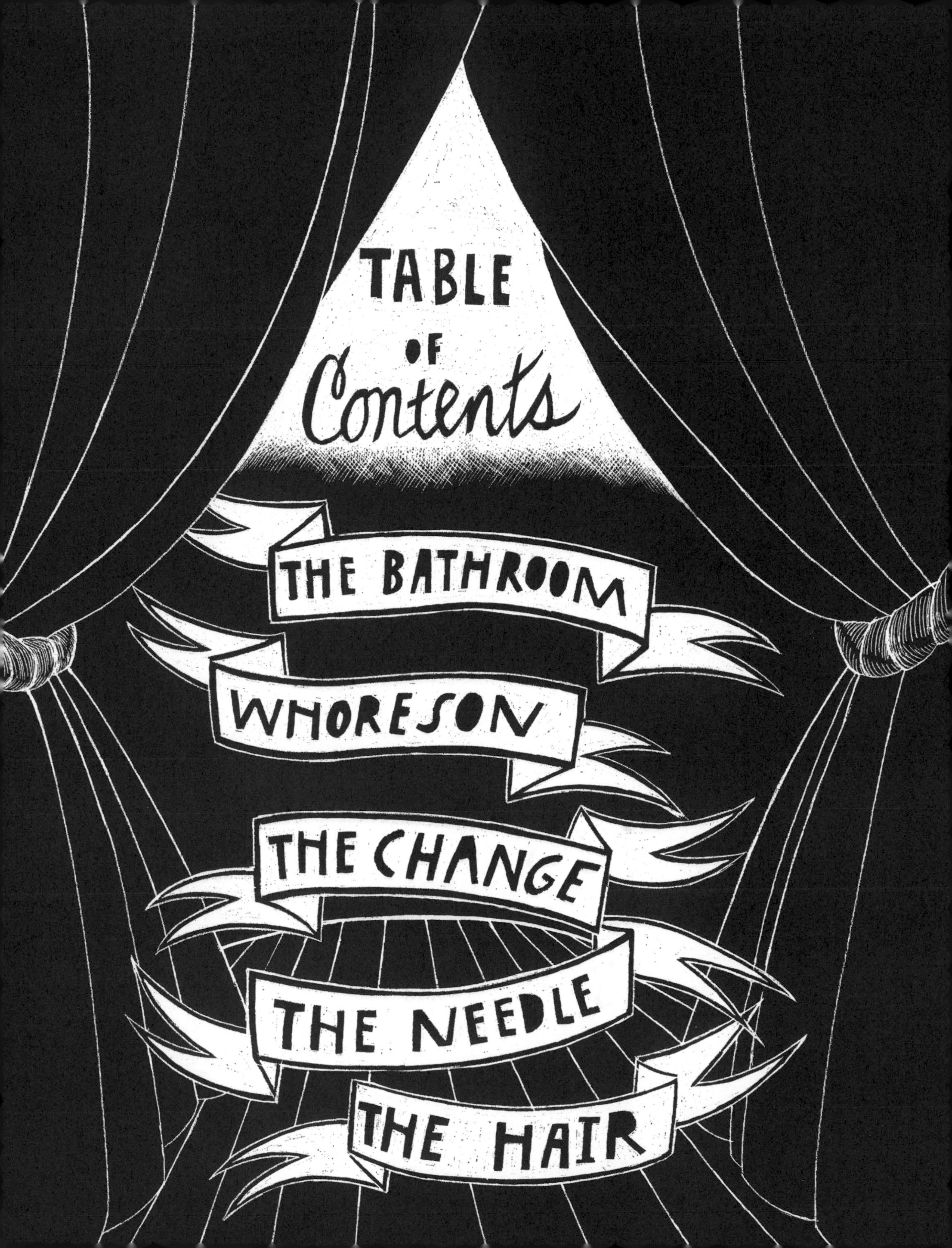
TABLE of Contents
THE BATHROOM
WHORESON
THE CHANGE
THE NEEDLE
THE HAIR

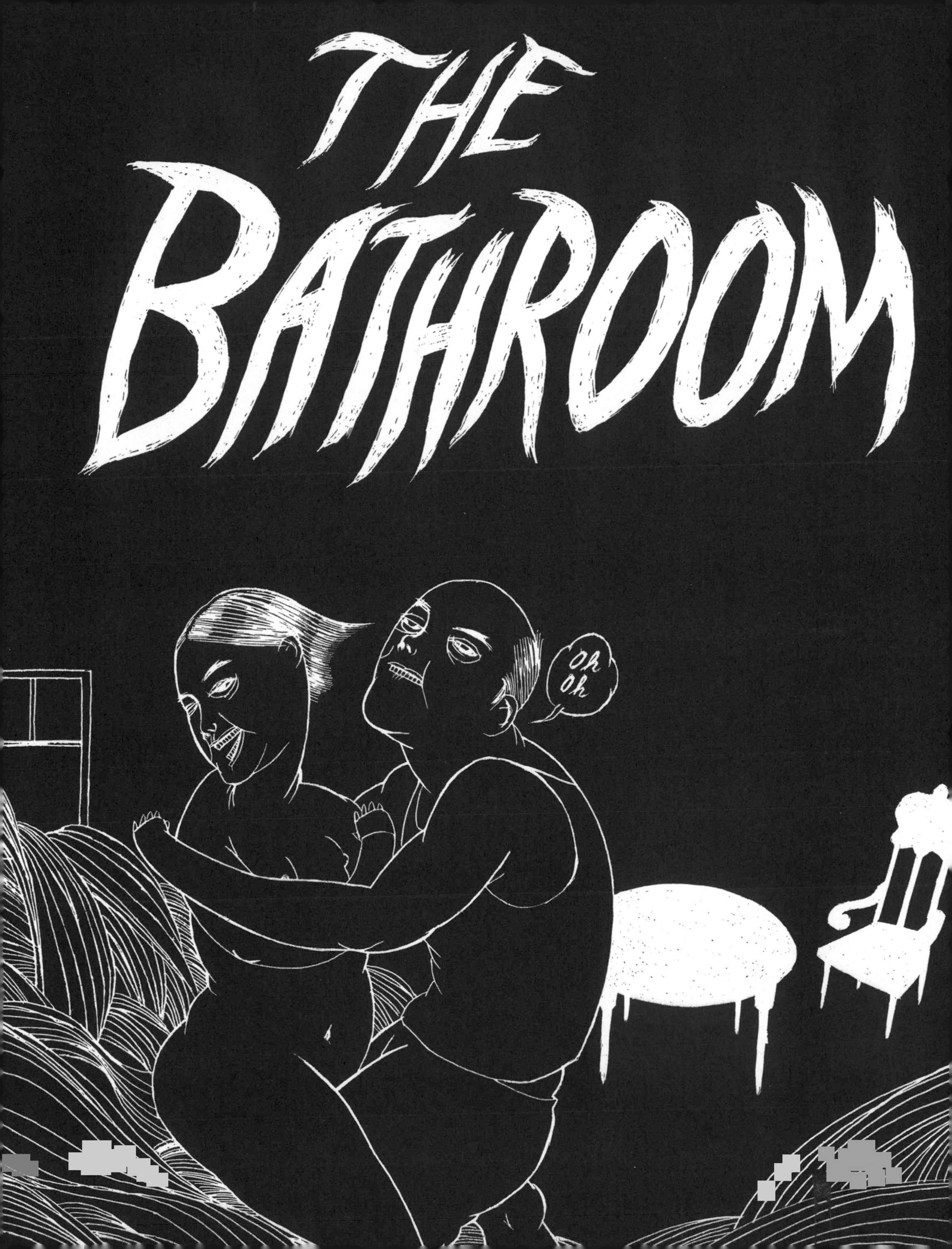
THE BATHROOM
Oh Oh

"I'M SORRY," SAID MRS. PAPER.
MR. PAPER WAS ASLEEP IN BED NEXT TO MRS. PAPER. HE
RECOGNIZED HIS WIFE'S VOICE THROUGH A COMPLICATED DREAM
HE WAS HAVING. "I'M SORRY, TOO." HE SAID, SLEEPING.
MR. AND MRS. PAPER HAD NEVER LOVED ANYONE ELSE.

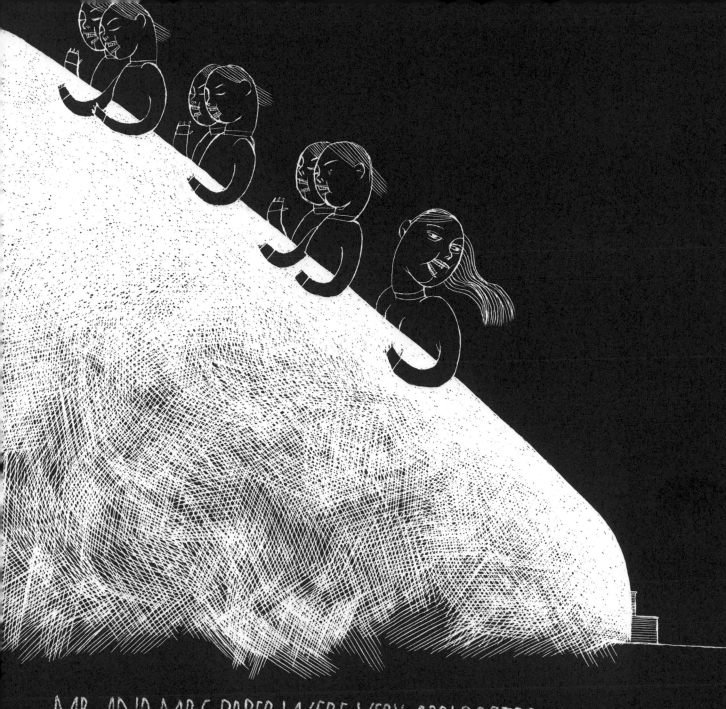

MR. AND MRS. PAPER WERE VERY APOLOGETIC. THEY
WERE THE MOST APOLOGETIC PEOPLE ANYONE HAD EVER
SEEN. MR. PAPER WAS AN ESCALATOR REPAIR MAN, AND
MRS. PAPER WAS A WRITER. SHE WROTE A MONTHLY
COLUMN IN HER COMMUNITY NEWSPAPER CALLED,
"PARADE OF THIEVES" ABOUT DOCTORS AND THE CORPORATIONS
THAT OWN HOSPITALS. MR. AND MRS. PAPER HAD MET
TWENTY YEARS AGO ON A MALL ESCALATOR, WHEN SHE
WAS GOING UP, AND HE WAS GOING DOWN.

ONCE, THE PAPERS HAD TRIED TO HAVE A CHILD, BUT THE PREGNANCY HAD CAUSED SUCH DEPRESSION AND RAGE FOR MRS. PAPER THAT THE BABY HAD COME OUT WRONG. THEY NAMED IT DANIEL, AND HELD IT UNTIL IT DIED, ON THE SECOND DAY. MRS. PAPER APOLOGIZED FOR CAUSING THE DOCTORS ANY TROUBLE, AND THEY WENT HOME AFTER FILLING OUT SEVERAL HOURS OF PAPERWORK.
ON THEIR 20TH ANNIVERSARY, MR. PAPER BOUGHT MRS. PAPER A SWIMMING POOL. MRS. PAPER GAVE HIM A STEEL WATCH.

MR. AND MRS. PAPER LIKED TO SWIM WHICH WAS SOMETHING THAT THEY DID TOGETHER. THEY SWAM EVERY DAY.

THERE WAS A DARK BROWN BIRCH TREE THAT DEEPENED THE LIGHT OF THEIR YARD AND HUNG OVER THE POOLHOUSE, WHERE THE PAPERS CHANGED. THE VERY FIRST SUMMER THAT THEY HAD THE POOL, A LOCAL BOY FELL AND DROWNED IN THE WATER. HE HAD FALLEN IN WHILE TRYING TO CLIMB THE BIRCH. WHEN THE PAPERS FOUND HIM, HE WAS VERY SUNBURNT. MRS PAPER'S NEXT COLUMN IN THE COMMUNITY JOURNAL WAS NOT AT ALL ABOUT HOSPITALS, BUT RATHER A DEEPLY REGRETFUL LETTER TO THE BOY'S FAMILY. THE POOL WAS THEN COVERED WITH A TARP. THE PAPERS NEVER SWAM AGAIN AFTER THAT. YEARS LATER, WHEN THE POOL WAS DUG UP AND TAKEN AWAY, NEW FAMILIES WOULD LAY THEMSELVES OUT IN THE BACKYARD WHILE TEENAGERS TRIPPED AND SWAYED OVER ONE ANOTHER IN ORDER TO DO ON A DESPERATE LAWN.

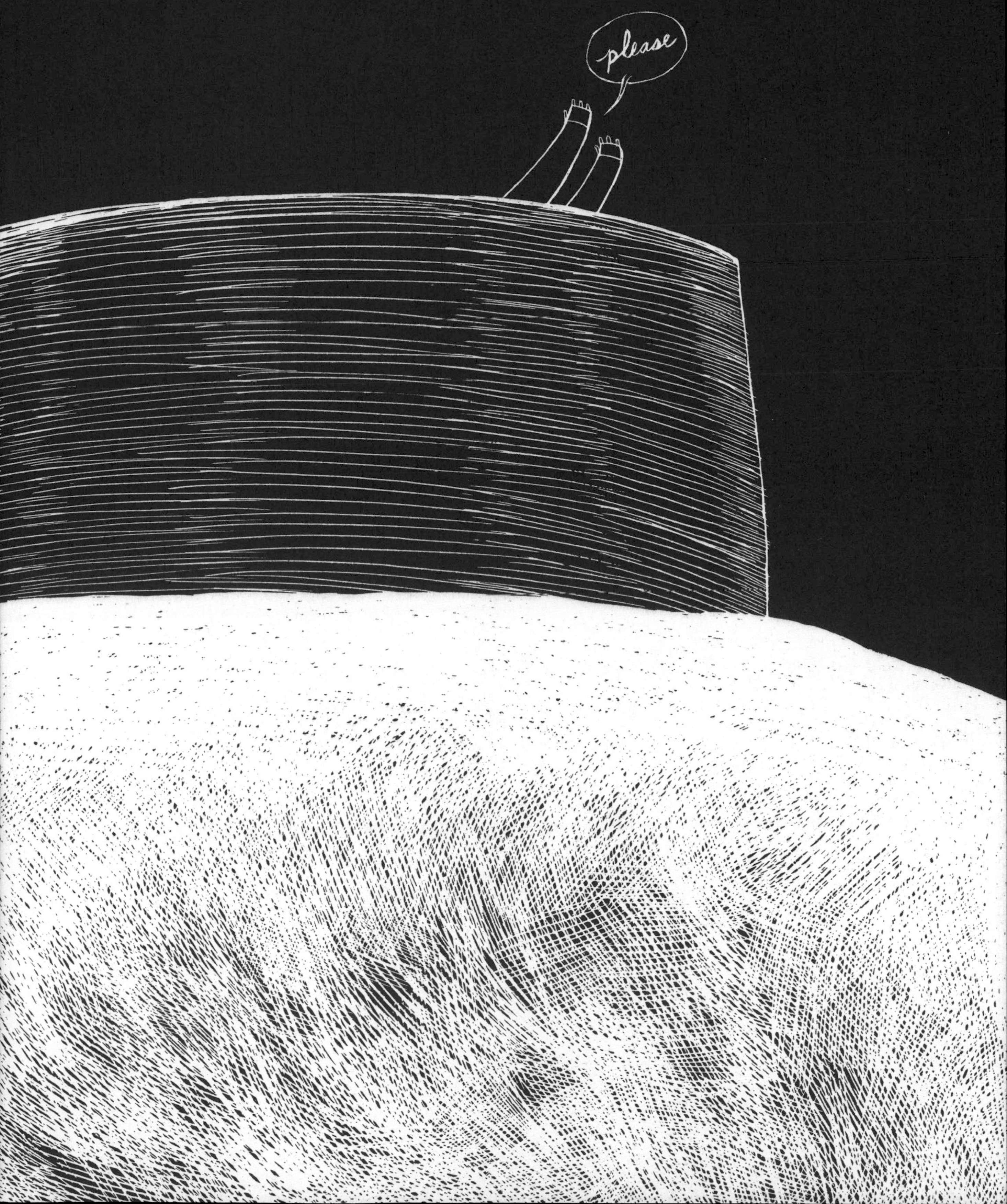
please

ONE AFTERNOON, WHILE HE WAS LOOKING FOR A SPECIAL KIND OF SCISSOR, MR. PAPER FOUND A SMALL HOLE IN THE FLOORBOARD OF THE POOLHOUSE. MRS. PAPER TOLD HIM IT WAS NOT WORTH FIXING SINCE THEY NO LONGER USED THE POOL. MR. PAPER SAID HE WAS SORRY TO HAVE BOTHERED HER, AND WOULD SHE LIKE TO GO TO A MOVIE. THEY SAW A FILM CALLED, "TORTURE ISLAND," AND CAME HOME TIRED.

WHEN THEY WERE FINISHING DINNER THE NEXT NIGHT, MR. PAPER SAW A LIGHT COMING FROM THE POOLHOUSE. "MAYBE IT'S A FIRE," SAID MRS. PAPER. SHE STAYED INSIDE AND WATCHED MR. PAPER WALK ACROSS THE DARK GRASS. WHEN HE WAS INSIDE THE POOLHOUSE, SHE BEGAN THE DISHES.

MR. PAPER SAW THAT THE LIGHT WAS COMING FROM THE HOLE IN THE FLOORBOARD. THE LIGHT WAS WARM AND LIMP. MR. PAPER WAS GLAD THAT IT WAS NOT RATS OR FIRE. WHEN HE PUT HIS FACE TO THE HOLE, HE SAW THAT IT WAS VERY DEEP, AND THAT THE LIGHT WAS COMING FROM FAR AWAY. THERE WAS ALSO A SMALL BIT OF SOUND COMING FROM THE HOLE.

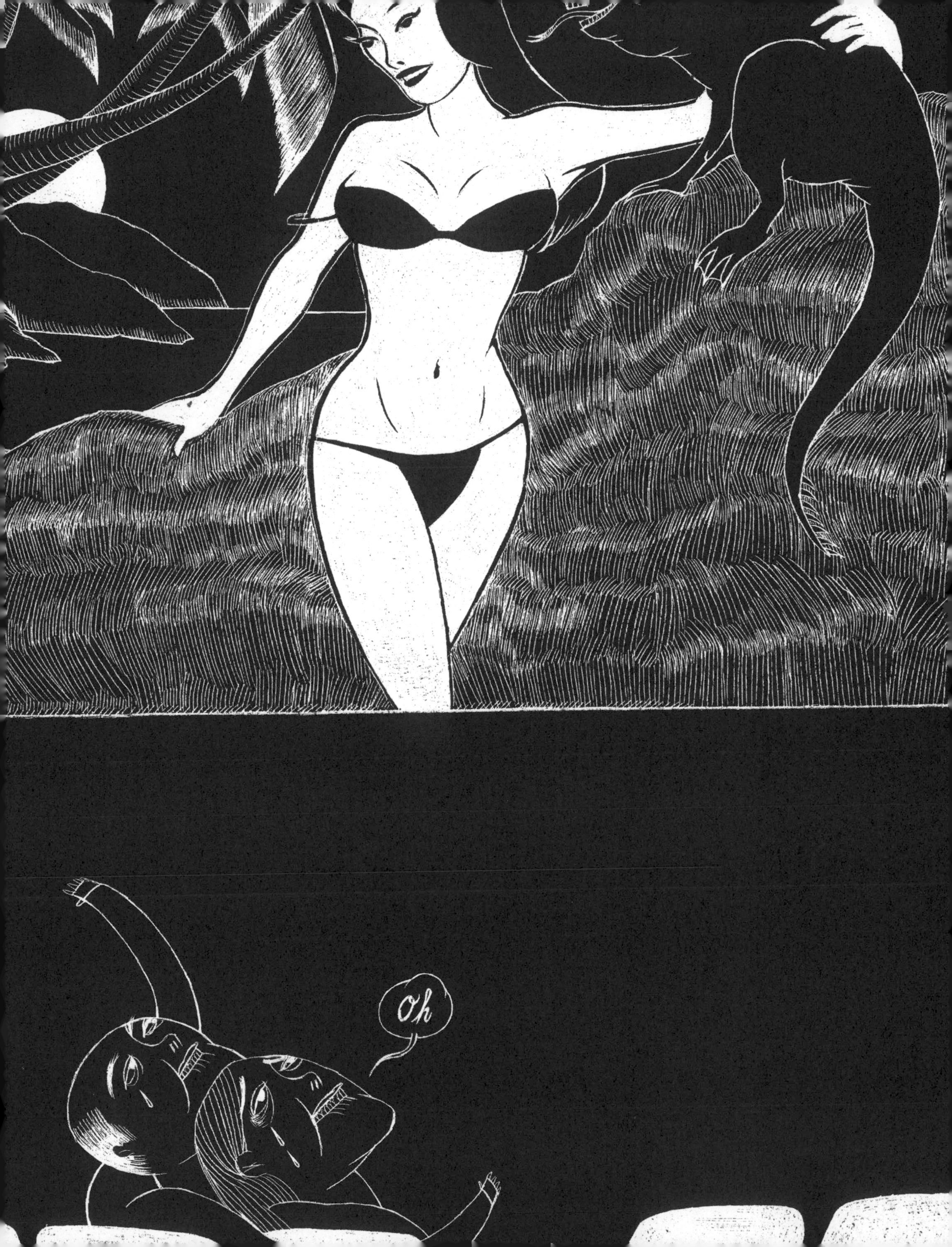
Oh

BY THE TIME MR. PAPER HAD TAKEN UP THE HEAVY FLOORBOARDS, MRS.
PAPER HAD ALREADY COME OUTSIDE. SHE WAS HOLDING A PHONEBOOK,
IN CASE IT HAD BEEN RATS. TOGETHER THEY SEPARATED ENOUGH BOARDS
TO SEE INTO A LONG BROWN TUNNEL. THE PAPERS PUSHED MOST
OF THEIR ARMS INTO THE HOLE, AND THEN THEIR BODIES. IT WAS
NOT VERY DARK.
THE TUNNEL WAS STRAIGHT AND CLEAN, AND THEY WALKED FOR 25
MINUTES TOWARD NOTHING. THEN THERE WAS NO SOUND AT ALL
EXCEPT FOR THE SOUND OF MRS. PAPER, WHO WAS BREATHING APOLOGETICALLY.
MR. PAPER THOUGHT ABOUT HOW FAR DOWN AND AWAY THEY MIGHT
BE. AFTER A WHILE, THEY CAME TO A WALL AND A VERY NICE-
LOOKING DOOR. IN DIFFICULT SCRIPT A SIGN READ, "POWDER ROOM."
THERE WAS NO MORE TUNNEL AFTER THAT. MRS. PAPER LOOKED AT
HER HUSBAND, AND THEN OPENED THE DOOR. INSIDE WAS A LARGE,
BLACK-AND WHITE EMPIRE TILE BATHROOM. IT WAS THE MOST
ELEGANT BATHROOM THEY HAD EVER SEEN.

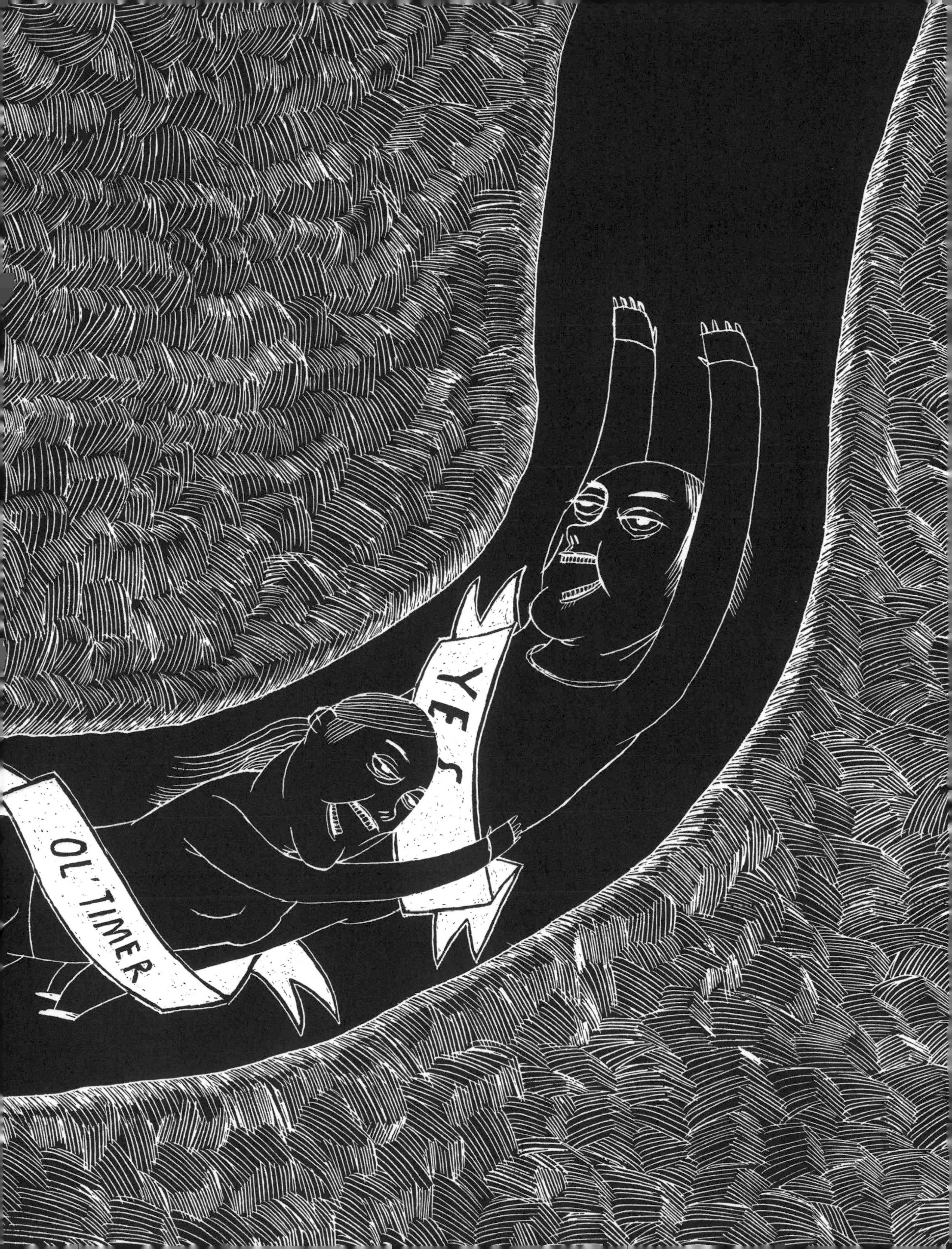
YES
OL' TIMER

THE NEXT DAY IT HAD RAINED A GREAT DEAL AND THERE WAS MUD IN THE TUNNEL. MR. PAPER WORE GALOSHES, AND MRS. PAPER SLIPPED SEVERAL TIMES GOING DOWN. THE BATHROOM WAS HUMID AND RUNNY. SLICK TILE MADE THE PIPES SHINE AND BULGE FROM BENEATH THE SINKS. THERE WERE 4 SINKS AGAINST ONE WALL, AND A MARBLE VANITY EQUIPPED WITH SUCH A LONG, LUSTROUS SURFACE THAT MRS. PAPER COULD HARDLY STOP HERSELF FROM BRUSHING HER HAIR WITH A NEARBY PEARL-HANDLED COMB. DELICATE FIXTURES BLOSSOMED FROM PRIVATE WHITE CABINETS, AND A MIRROR AS WIDE AS AN ENTIRE WALL PERSPIRED GENTLY IN THE WET HEAT. MANY DRAWERS COVERED SOME LOW TABLES, GLOWING IMPORTANTLY DESPITE THEIR LACK OF SERIOUS PURPOSE.

MR. PAPER DECIDED TO TOUCH THE CEILING AND WALLS TO SEE IF HE COULD DISCOVER ANYTHING. HE TOUCHED AROUND THE ROOM AND FELT SOLID THINGS. AT ONE SPOT ALONG THE CEILING, THERE WAS A GRAND LAMP, WHICH MR. PAPER TOUCHED AS WELL. A LOUD CRACK WAS HEARD, AND THE BASE OF THE LAMP GAVE WAY FROM THE CEILING TILES, AND CAUSED A HOLE TO FORM ABOVE THEIR HEADS. THE PAPERS SAW DIRT AND FOUNDATION THROUGH THE HOLE. THEY STOOD ON A CHAIR AND BEGAN TO DIG.

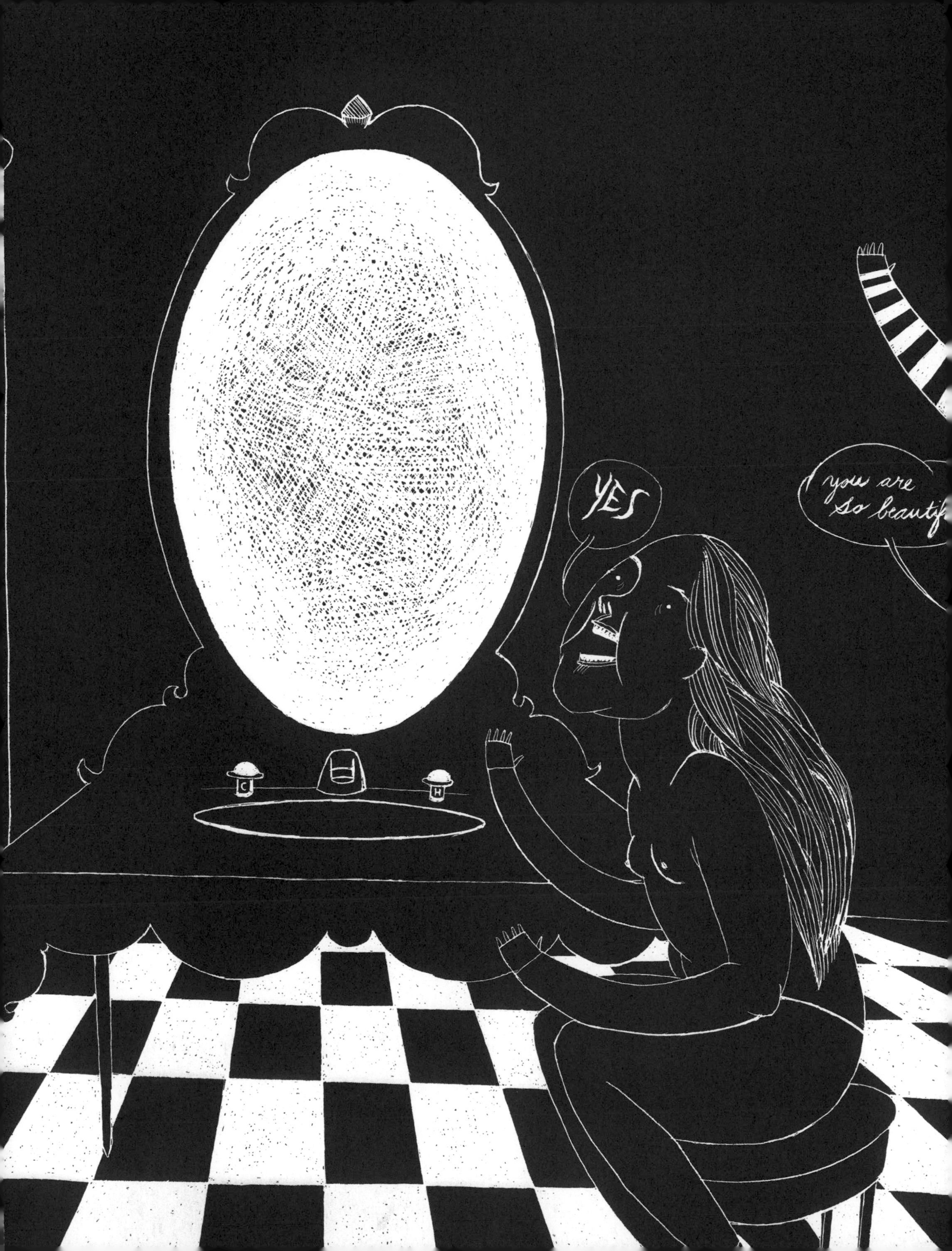
YES
you are so beautif

GREAT CLUMPS OF DIRT FELL INTO THEIR FACES AND HANDS.
THEY HIT AN ALUMINUM PIPE AND SOME CEMENT. "IT MUST
BE OUR POOL," SAID MR. PAPER. "OH YES," SAID MRS. PAPER. THEY DUG
AND DUG AND SOON THEY HAD MADE A SQUARE THAT LOOKED OUT ONTO
DIRT.
WHEN A LONG TIME HAD PASSED AND THE POOL-BOTTOM WAS
ALMOST ENTIRELY EXPOSED, THEY HEARD A SOUND BEHIND ONE
OF THE STALL DOORS. MR. PAPER STOPPED DIGGING AND LOOKED
AT MRS. PAPER, WHO LOOKED VERY MUCH LIKE THE WHITE TILE.
THERE WAS A SOUND LIKE TALKING COMING FROM THE STALL. MR.
PAPER WENT TO THE DOOR WHICH BULGED WITH NOISE. MRS.
PAPER BEGAN TO SCREAM, AS RECOGNITION CLUTCHED HER FACE.
"OH NO," SAID MR. PAPER. MRS. PAPER BEGAN TO CRY. THEY HAD ONLY
KNOWN THE BOY WHO DROWNED SLIGHTLY, FROM THE SOUND OF HIS
VOICE IN THEIR NEIGHBOR'S YARD. THE TALKING FROM THE STALL WAS
VERY CALM AND QUIET. THE DOOR OF THE STALL WAS LOCKED.
ABOVE THEM, CEILING-DIRT BEGAN TO GIVE WAY AND FALL. "WE
SHOULD LEAVE NOW," SAID MR. PAPER. HEAVY MUD RUSHED INTO
THE ROOM. "YES," SAID MRS. PAPER.

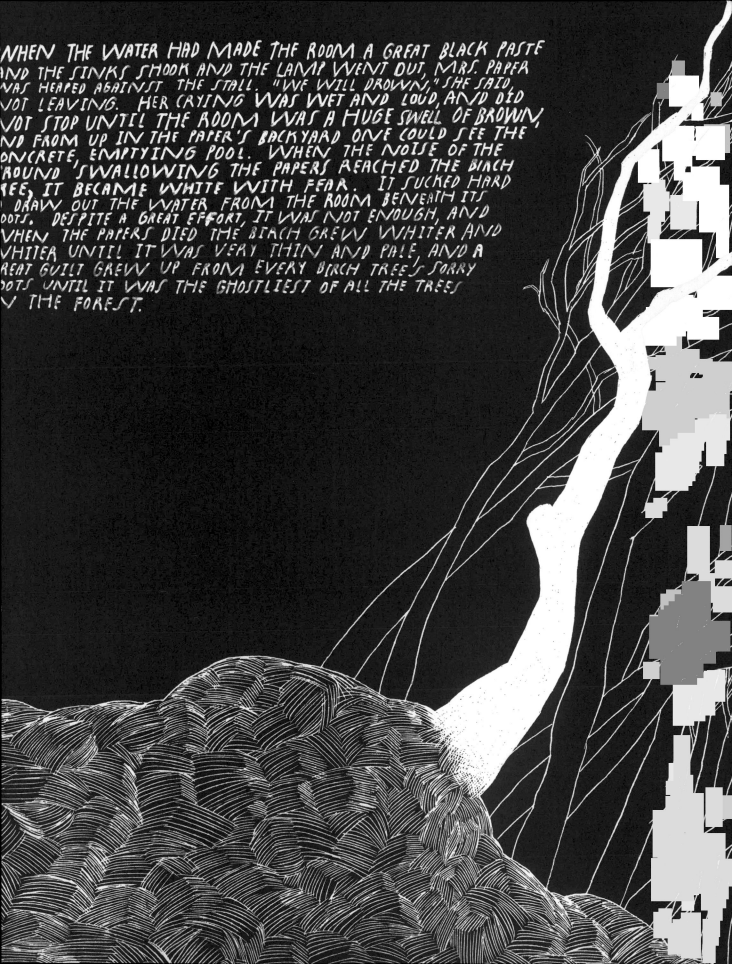

WHEN THE WATER HAD MADE THE ROOM A GREAT BLACK PASTE AND THE SINKS SHOOK AND THE LAMP WENT OUT, MRS. PAPER WAS HEAPED AGAINST THE STALL. "WE WILL DROWN," SHE SAID, NOT LEAVING. HER CRYING WAS WET AND LOUD, AND DID NOT STOP UNTIL THE ROOM WAS A HUGE SWELL OF BROWN, AND FROM UP IN THE PAPER'S BACKYARD ONE COULD SEE THE CONCRETE, EMPTYING POOL. WHEN THE NOISE OF THE GROUND SWALLOWING THE PAPERS REACHED THE BIRCH TREE, IT BECAME WHITE WITH FEAR. IT SUCKED HARD TO DRAW OUT THE WATER FROM THE ROOM BENEATH ITS ROOTS. DESPITE A GREAT EFFORT, IT WAS NOT ENOUGH, AND WHEN THE PAPERS DIED THE BIRCH GREW WHITER AND WHITER UNTIL IT WAS VERY THIN AND PALE, AND A GREAT GUILT GREW UP FROM EVERY BIRCH TREE'S SORRY ROOTS UNTIL IT WAS THE GHOSTLIEST OF ALL THE TREES IN THE FOREST.

END

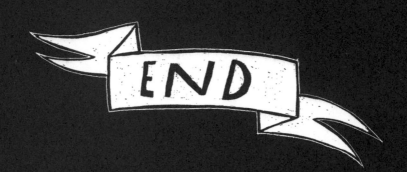

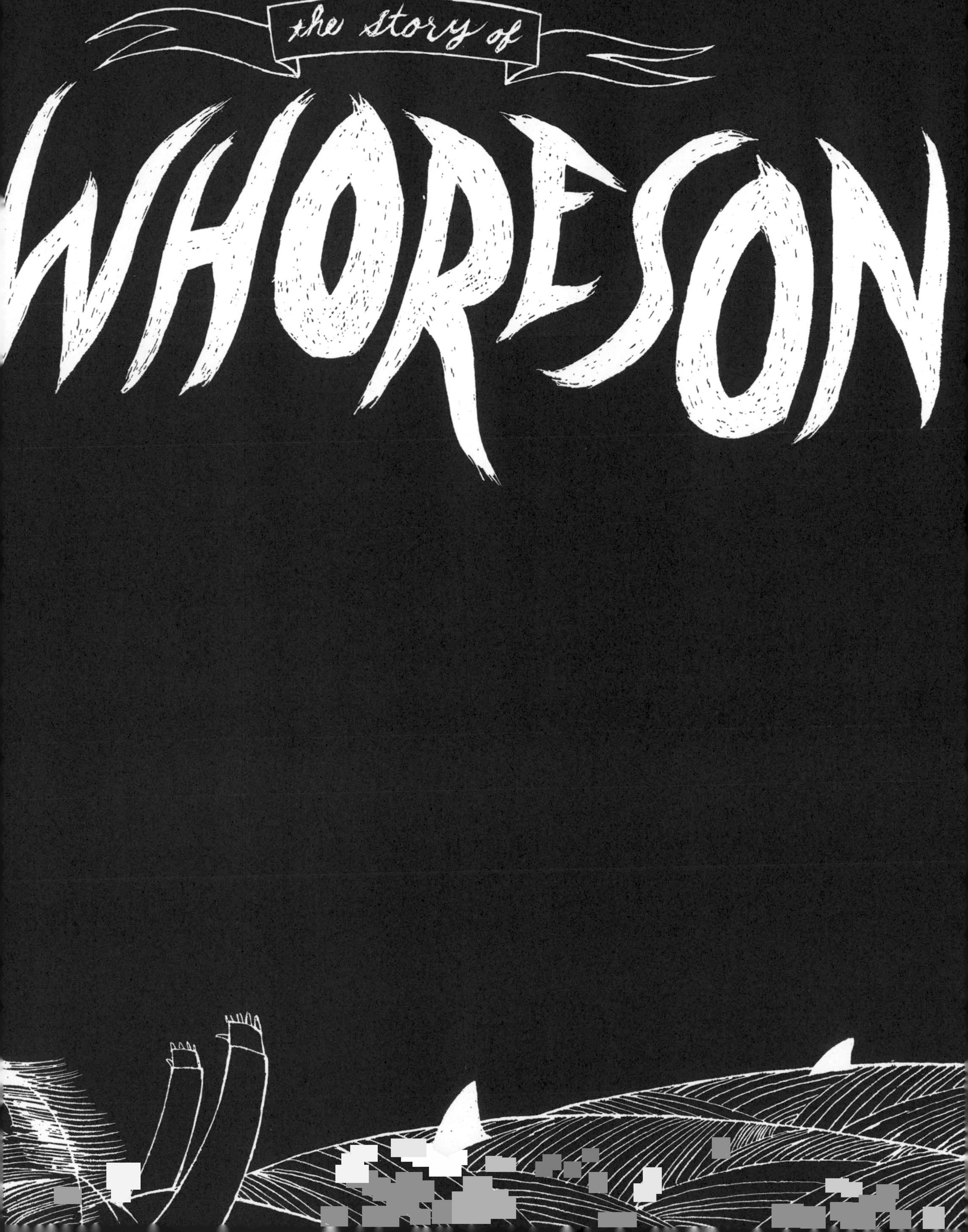
the story of
WHORESON

ONCE UPON A TIME THERE WAS A MAN NAMED WHORESON.
HE HAD HAIR ALL OVER HIS FACE AND BODY, EVEN UP TO HIS EYES,
LIKE A BEAST. WHORESON LIVED IN NEW HAMPSHIRE, AND
WHEN HE WEPT OR ATE, HE BECAME MATTED. HE HAD A GIRLFRIEND,
AND EVEN THOUGH NEW ENGLAND WAS VERY COLD, WHORESON
WAS ALWAYS WARM. HIS MOTHER, ELENOR, HAD NEVER HAD
A HUSBAND AND LIVED SOMEWHERE IN SOME CITY.

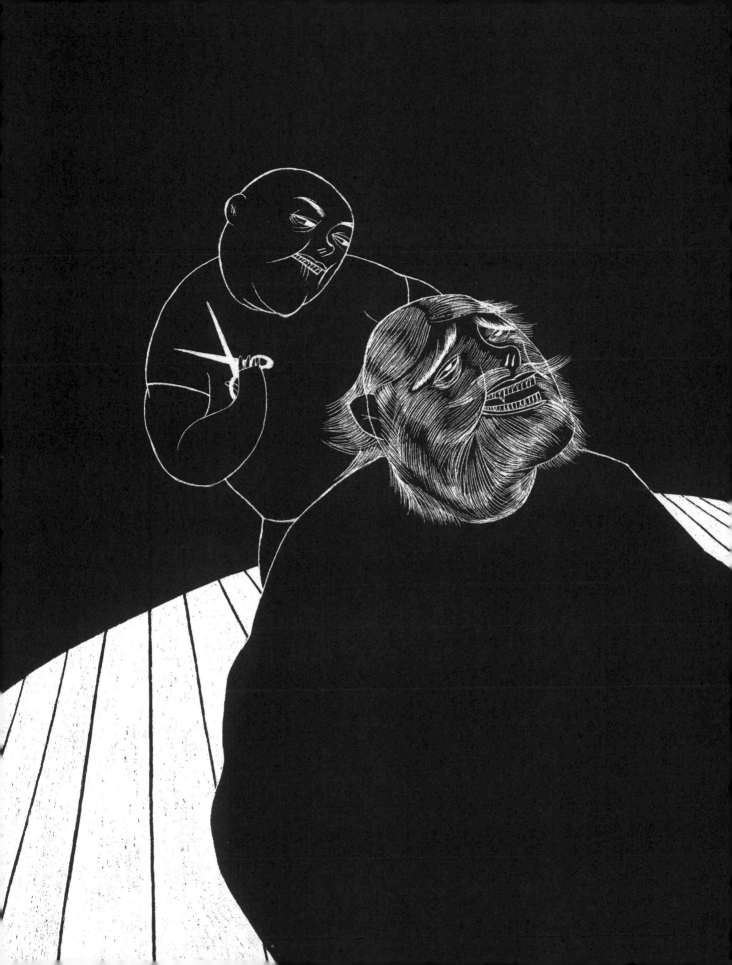

WHORESON BELIEVED THAT PEOPLE WERE UNDERSTANDING, SO HE UNDERSTOOD EVERYBODY. HIS GIRLFRIEND HAD A GARDEN AT THE BOTTOM OF THEIR DRIVEWAY. SOMETIMES SHE WOULD FIND STRINGS AND STRANDS OF HIS HAIR AMONG THE WEEDS WHILE SHE WAS GARDENING. ONE OF THE INTERESTING THINGS ABOUT WHORESON WAS THAT HE HAD TWO HEARTS, ONE ON EITHER SIDE OF HIS CHEST.

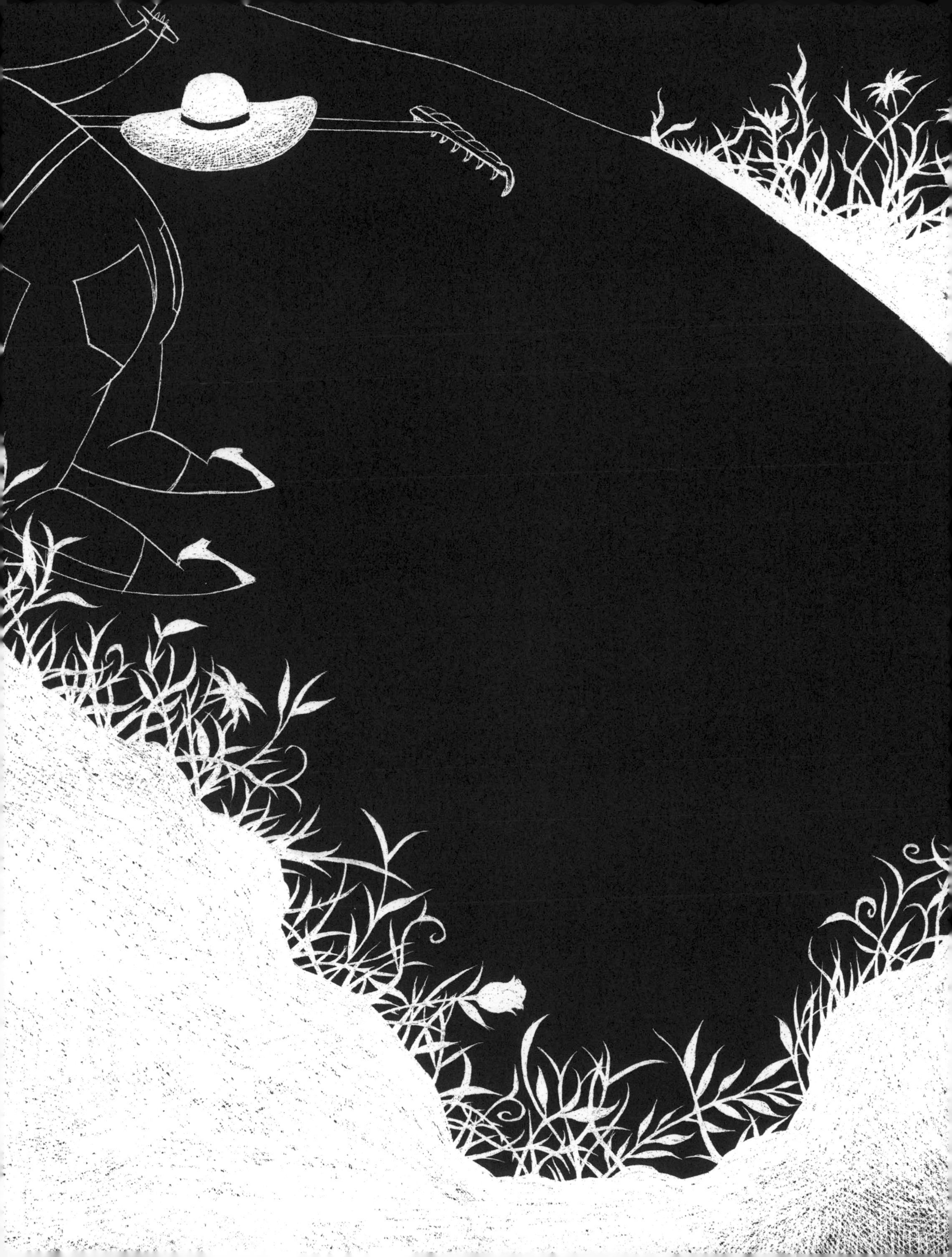

WHEN HE WAS IN COLLEGE, WHORESON MAJORED IN ECONOMICS. IT WAS WHERE HE MET HIS GIRLFRIEND. AFTER A CERTAIN AMOUNT OF TIME, THEY DID NOT HIDE THEIR RELATIONSHIP.

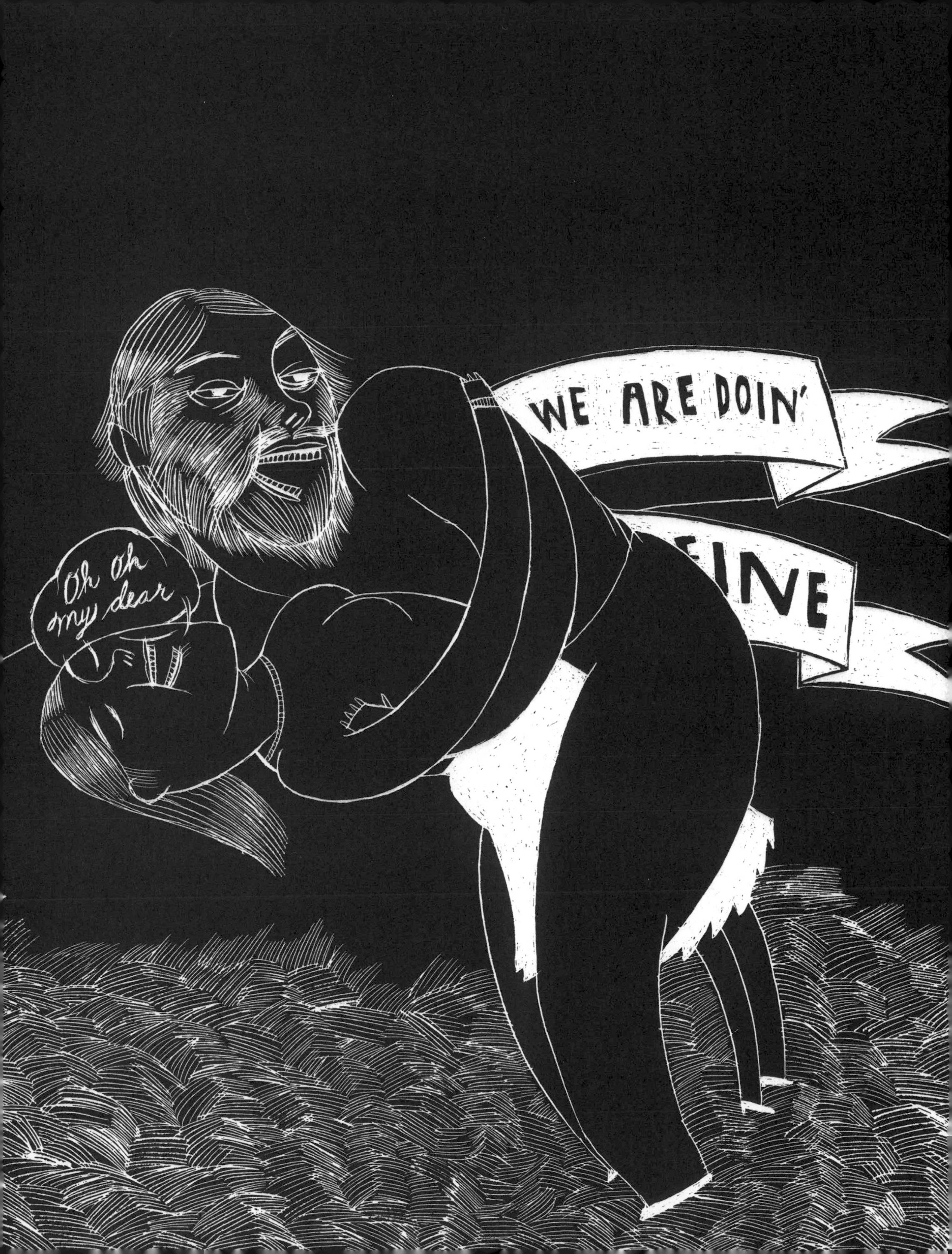
WE ARE DOIN'
FINE
Oh oh
my dear

SOMETIMES BOYS WITH BIG EYES WOULD SLIP THEIR ARMS AROUND WHORESON'S GIRLFRIEND DURING ECONOMICS CLASS AND WHISPER VERY CLOSE TO HER NECK. "LOOK AT WHORESON," THEY WOULD SAY, "HOW CAN A MONSTER HOLD YOU." OR, "HE MUST BE A VERY GROSS FUCK." ONCE, A BOY THREW A BOOK AT WHORESON AND CUT HIM ON THE FACE. BLOOD ON WHORESON LOOKS SLICK AND BLACK AND WET.

WHEN HE WAS OLDER AND LIVING IN NEW HAMPSHIRE, WHORESON
DECIDED TO WRITE A BOOK ABOUT HIS HAIR AND FACE. IT WAS
CALLED "THE OUTING", AND WAS ABOUT BEING A BEAST. HE
FOUND A SENSITIVE EDITOR, AND THE BOOK BECAME FAIRLY FAMOUS
RIGHT AWAY. WHORESON WAS UNAFRAID, AND VERY PROUD OF IT.
HIS GIRLFRIEND CAME TO ALL OF HIS BOOK SIGNINGS, AND LATER WHEN
HE WAS ASKED TO LECTURE AT HIS OLD UNIVERSITY, SHE ALSO WENT
WITH HIM.   THE SURPRISE ENDING OF THE BOOK WAS THAT WHORESON
HAD TWO HEARTS.
HE THEN TAUGHT FOR SEVERAL YEARS AT HIS UNIVERSITY, AND
MANY PEOPLE WERE MOVED.

ONE DAY WHORESON AND HIS GIRLFRIEND HAD A BABY. IT WAS A GIRL WITH VERY CLEAR SKIN. SHE WAS BORN TOO EARLY, AND DIED WHEN SHE WAS THE SIZE OF A BUSINESS LETTER. WHORESON CRIED AND SCREAMED AND DID NOT TEACH FOR A LONG TIME.

WHEN HIS GIRLFRIEND WANTED ANOTHER BABY, WHORESON WORRIED FOR SEVEN STRAIGHT MONTHS AND ONE OF HIS HEARTS BECAME DISTENDED. THE DOCTOR SAID THAT IT WAS ALL RIGHT TO TRY, SO THEY DID. THE SECOND CHILD WAS A BOY, AND IT WAS ALSO NOT COVERED IN HAIR. THE GIRLFRIEND WAS VERY PROUD AND WHORESON WAS VERY PROUD, AND THEY BOTH FELT BETTER. THE BABY GREW UP A LITTLE UNTIL IT COULD FIT INSIDE WHORESON'S HANDS, AND THEN IT DIED. WHORESON DID NOT SPEAK FOR A YEAR AND MOVED WITH HIS GIRLFRIEND TO A HOUSE ON THE OCEAN. HE WROTE A BOOK ABOUT THE SEA, WHICH BECAME ANOTHER FAMOUS BOOK.

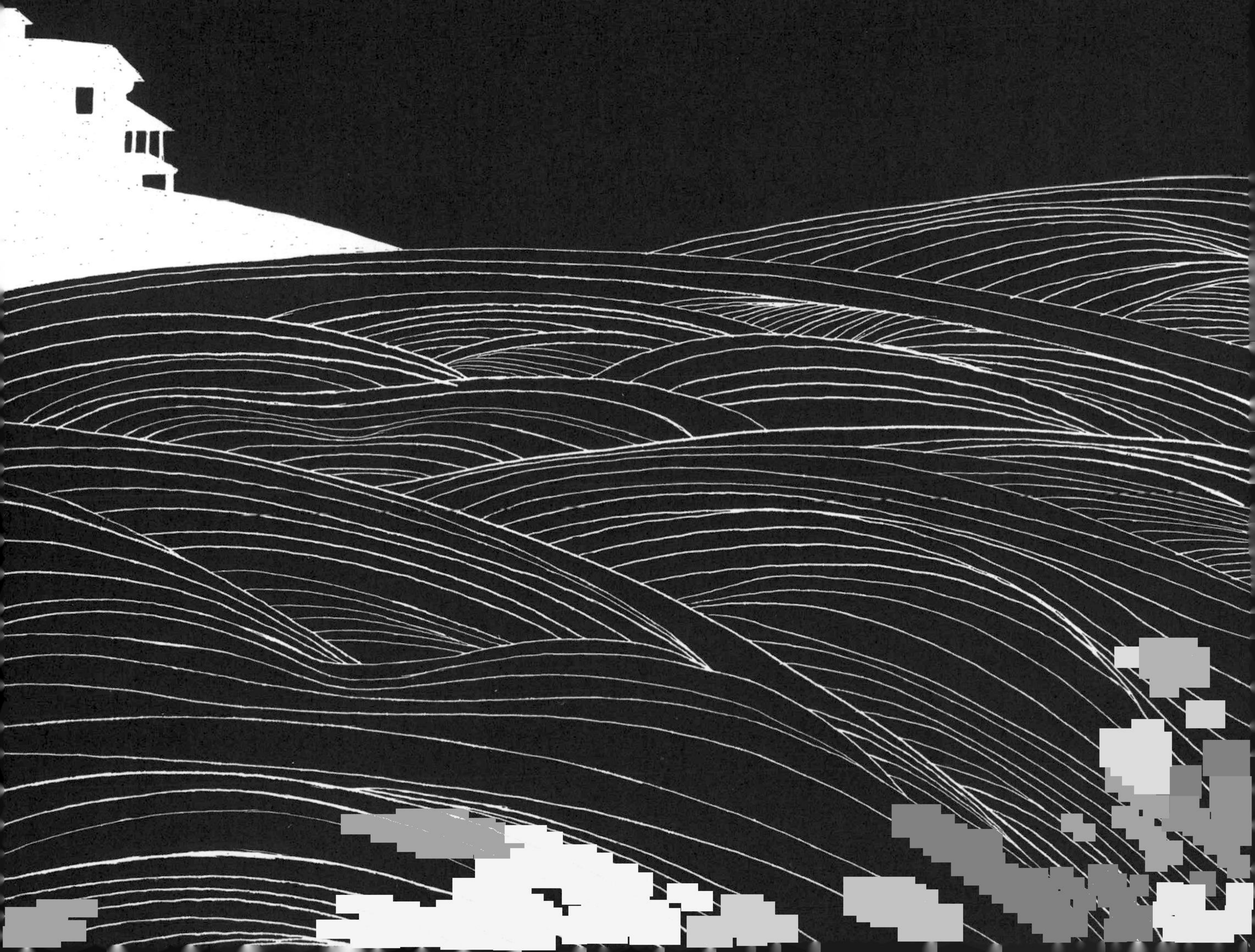

AFTER A WHILE, HIS GIRLFRIEND BECAME PREGNANT AGAIN. WHORESON
WAS CONCERNED AND HIS HAIR TURNED DIFFERENT COLORS OF WHITE
AND WAGGED IN THE SEA-WIND. WHEN THE THIRD CHILD WAS BORN
IT STAYED ALIVE AND GREW UNTIL IT WAS THE SIZE OF A PAIR OF
PANTS, AND WHORESON LOVED IT AND WROTE A BOOK CALLED,
"PERCEPTIBLE TRUTH" ABOUT HIS HAPPINESS. THE SON GREW UP
TO BE COVERED IN THICK HAIR, AND WAS VERY EMBARRASSED.
HE CRIED AT NIGHT AND THOUGHT HIS FATHER LOOKED LIKE A CREATURE.

WHEN HE CAME HOME FROM SCHOOL ONE DAY, THERE WERE A COUPLE OF
FANS OUTSIDE OF WHORESON'S HOUSE, LOOKING TO GET AN AUTOGRAPH.
"YOU ARE VERY LUCKY," SAID ONE STUDENT. "NO," SAID THE BOY, "I'M NOT."
HE LOOKED SAD AND HID HIS FACE WITH HIS HANDS. "HE IS A BEAUTIFUL
MAN," SAID AN ADMIRER. "HE IS A BEAST." SAID THE BOY.

WHORESON CAME OUT OF HIS HOUSE TO SEE HIS FANS AND HOLD HIS CHILD.
HIS EYES SHIVERED WITH HAPPINESS AT THE SIGHT OF THE BOY, AND
HIS HEARTS HULKED IN HIS CHEST. WHEN THE BOY SAW WHORESON,
HE DID NOT SMILE OR SHIVER. HE LOOKED AT HIS OWN COARSE
HAIR, THEN PICKED UP ONE OF HIS BROWN BOOKS AND THREW IT
AT THE BEAST. IT HIT WHORESON IN THE FACE SO HARD THAT
HE FELL AGAINST THE DRIVEWAY AND HIS SKULL BROKE AND HE
BLED TO DEATH RIGHT AWAY.
WHEN HIS HEARTS BURST, THE BLOOD FELL INTO THE WATER AND WARMED
IT SO THAT MANY FISH FROM ALL OVER BEGAN TO POPULATE THE OCEAN
AND THERE WAS AN ABUNDANCE OF FOOD AND THE TOWN BECAME VERY
RICH FOR A LONG TIME.

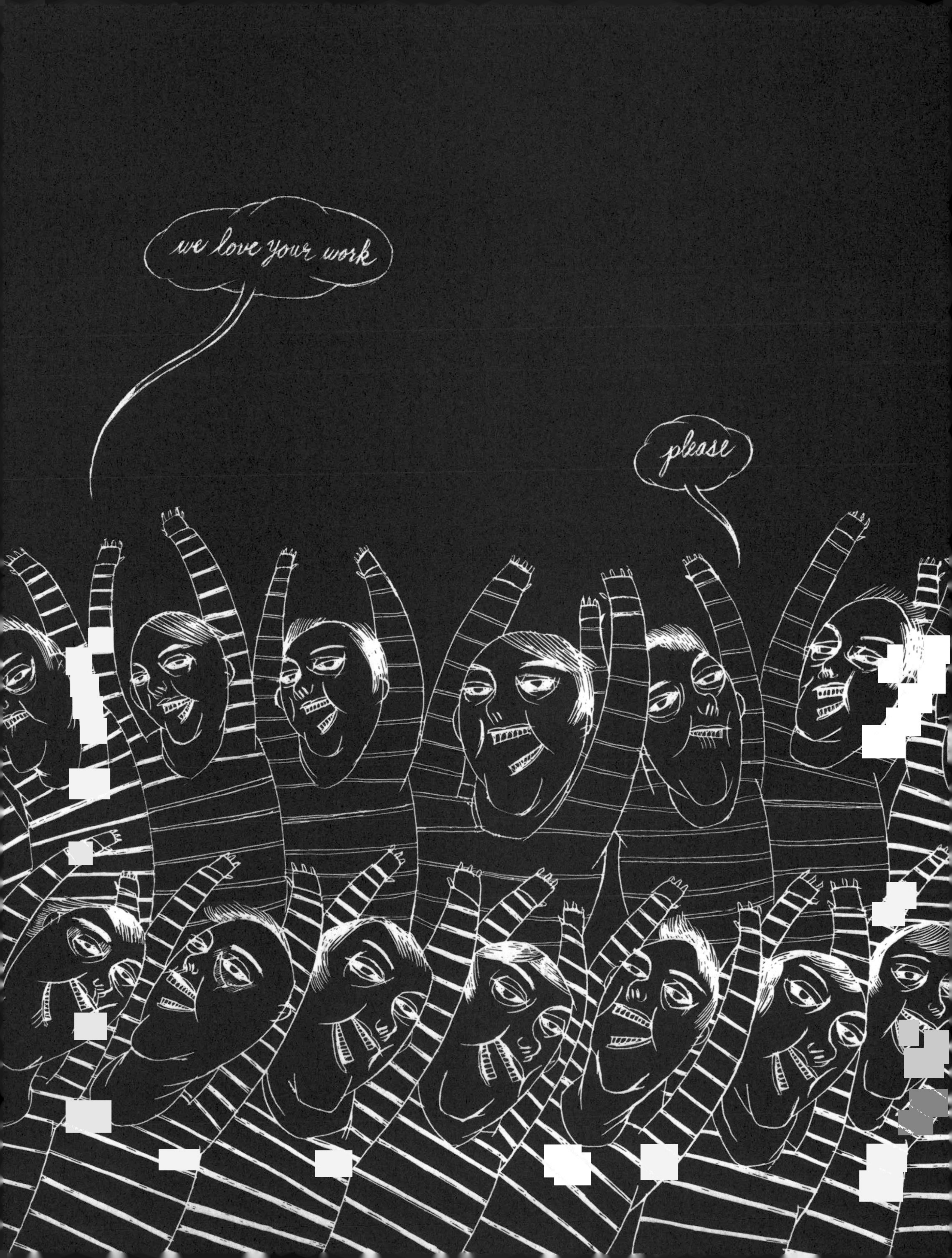
we love your work
please

THE FUNERAL WAS NEAR A PORT WHERE FISHING BOATS CAME AND DOCKED, AND HUNDREDS OF PEOPLE AND CHILDREN AND AUTHORS AND WHOLE UNIVERSITIES OF STUDENTS ALL CAME TO SEE WHORESON. HE WAS LAID OUT ON THE DOCK, AND HIS HAIR SLUMPED WITH DEATH. NEAR THE END OF THE SPEECHES, AN ANCIENT WOMAN PUSHED THROUGH THE PEOPLE. SHE WAS BENT ALMOST EXACTLY IN HALF WITH AGE. "SHE IS TOO OLD AND CANNOT SPEAK," WHISPERED THE CROWD. "IT IS HIS MOTHER," SOMEONE SAID. ELENOR WALKED TOWARDS THE CASKET, WHICH TOOK ONE WHOLE HOUR. WHEN SHE GOT THERE, SHE TOOK HUGE, BLACK STRANDS OF HER SON'S HAIR, AND HELD THEM IN HER MINUSCULE ARMS. "A BEAUTIFUL BOY," SAID THE WHORE, "MY BEAUTIFUL BOY".

YEARS LATER, THE WATERS AROUND THE PORT BECAME SO FILLED WITH FISH, AND THE TOWN BECAME SO RICH, THAT IT SOON WAS FAMOUS. EVENTUALLY THE WATER WAS OVERFLOWING WITH FISH, AND THEY BEGAN TO EAT EACH OTHER, UNTIL THE ONLY SPECIES LEFT WERE THOSE THAT WERE FIERCE AND FILLED WITH TEETH, LIKE SHARKS.

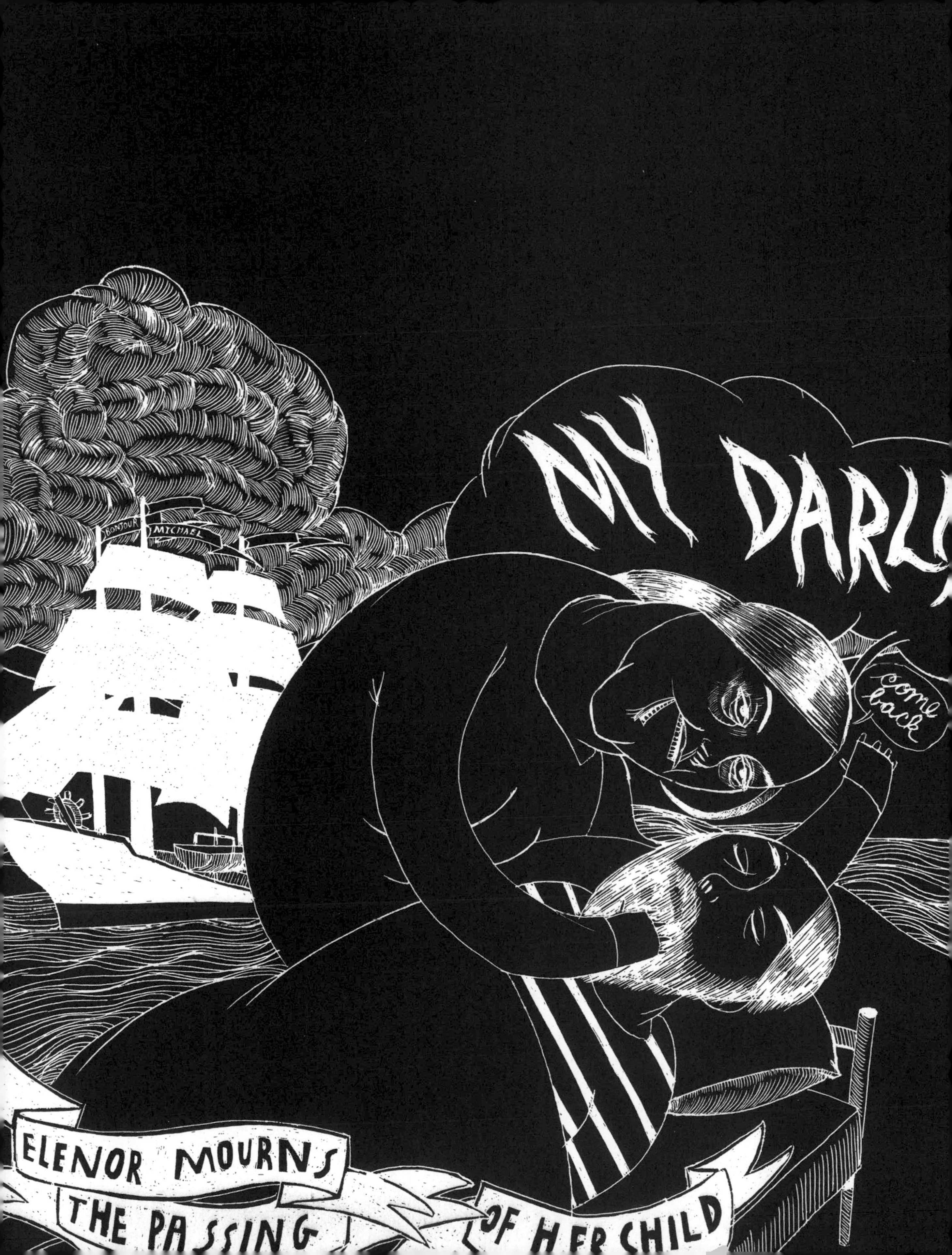
BONJOUR MICHAEL
MY DARLI
come back
ELENOR MOURNS
THE PASSING
OF HER CHILD

END

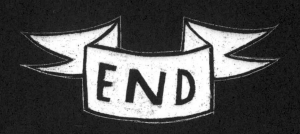

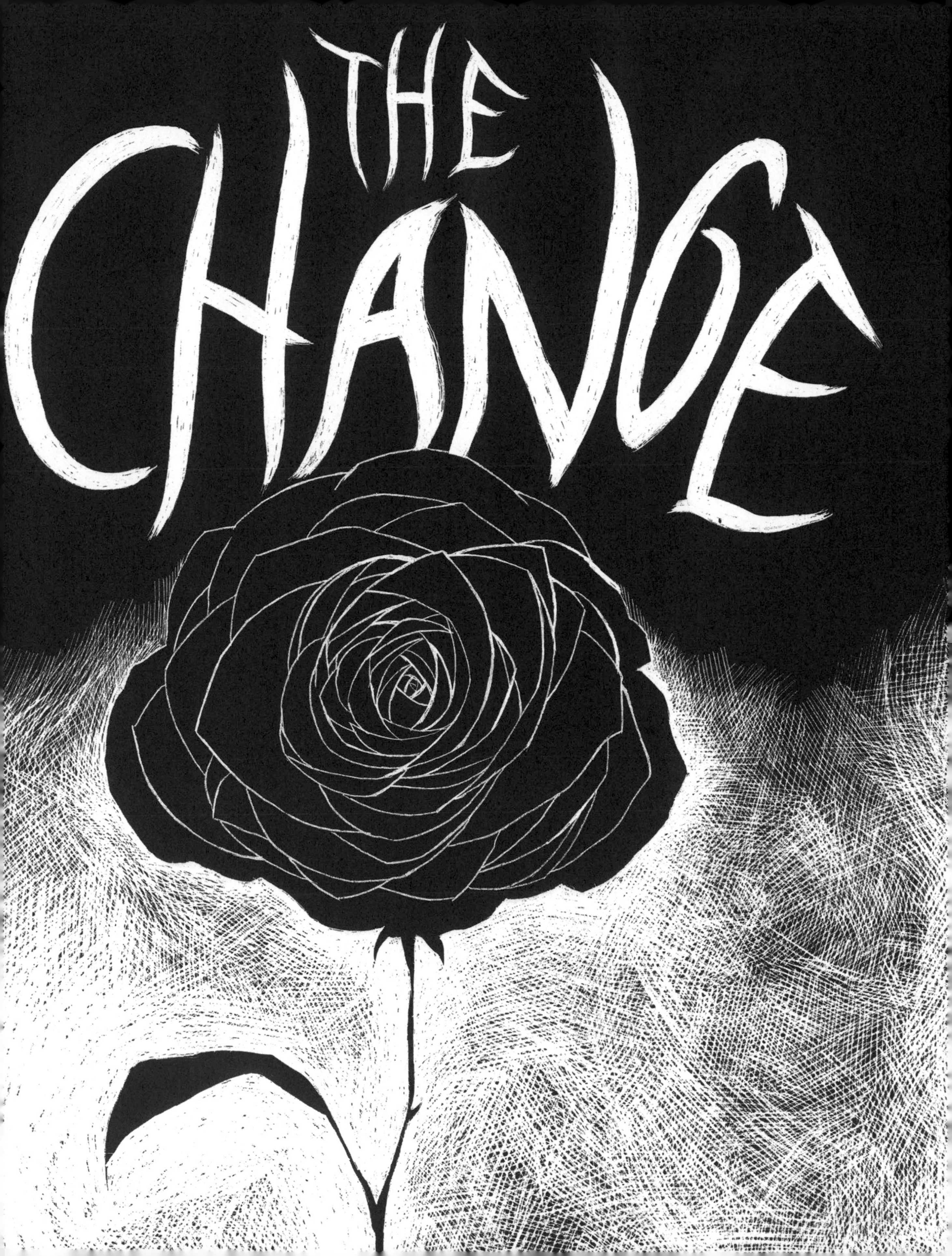
THE CHANGE

AT ONE TIME, JEREMY HAD BEEN A WONDERFUL PERSON.

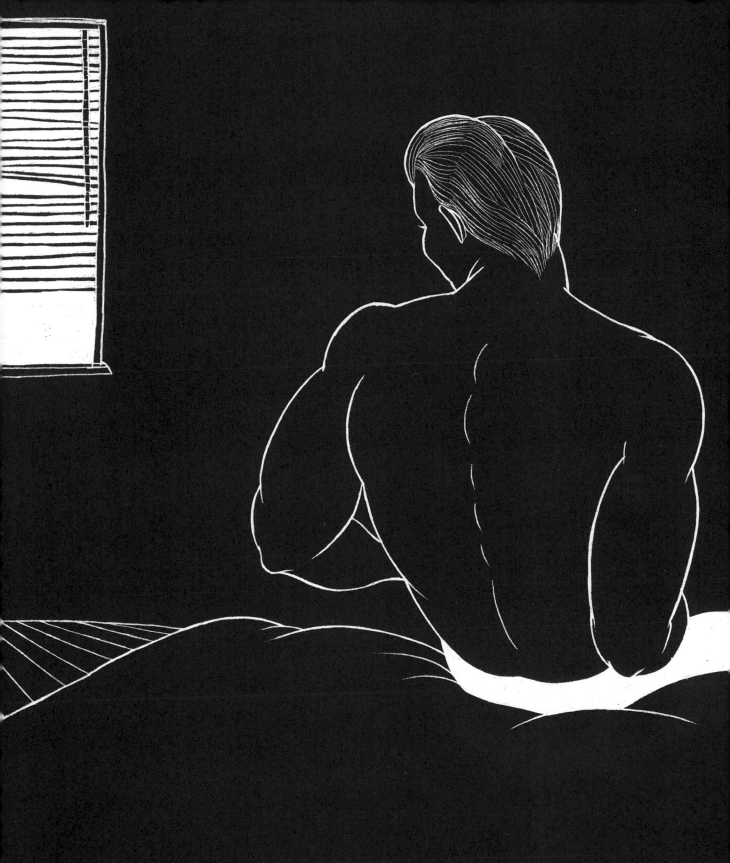

BACK THEN, HE WAS VERY STRONG, WITH BIG ARMS TO HOLD
PLATES AND DISHES. JEREMY WAS A WAITER AT A FAMOUS
RESTAURANT WHERE THEY SERVED A SPECIAL KIND OF DUCK.

THE DUCKS WERE KILLED FRESH EVERY SINGLE NIGHT. THAT WAS THE RESTAURANT'S SPECIALTY. IT WAS JEREMY'S JOB TO HOLD THE DUCK, STILL ALIVE, AND BRING IT TO THE TABLE FOR THE GUESTS TO SEE BEFORE COOKING IT. THE DUCK BEAT ITS WINGS AGAINST HIS FACE AND CHEST. HE WAITED AT THE TABLE WHILE THE MEN NODDED, AND THE WOMEN PINCHED THE FLESH FOR FAT. "YES," THEY'D SAY, "THIS IS FINE." JEREMY WAITED NO MATTER HOW LONG IT TOOK FOR THE CUSTOMERS TO DECIDE. SOMETIMES THEY ASKED HIM TO BRING OUT A NEW DUCK. THE ROOM WAS ALWAYS LOUD WITH THE SCREAMS OF ANIMALS BEING BROUGHT IN AND OUT OF THE KITCHEN. IT WAS A VERY EXPENSIVE RESTAURANT.

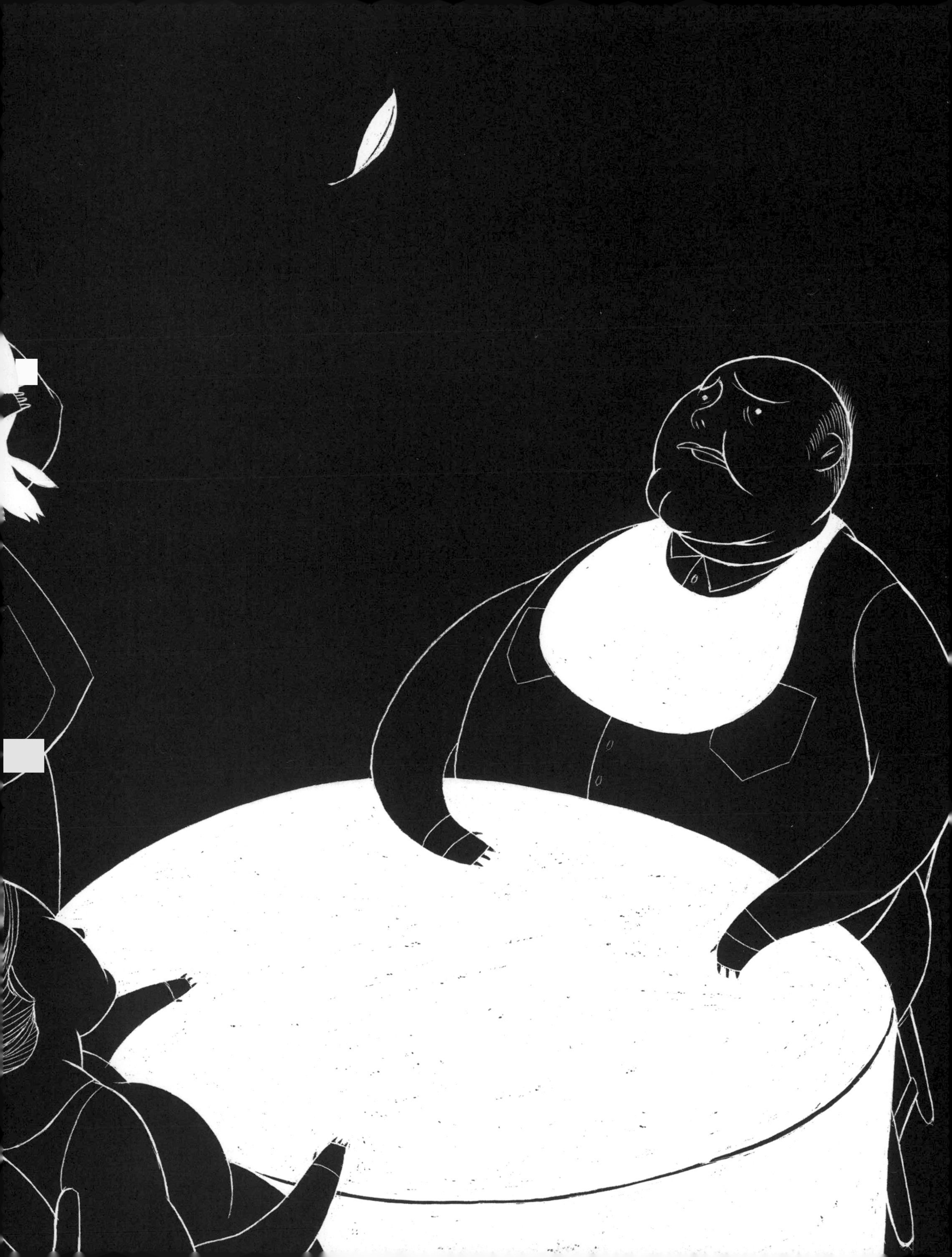

WHEN HE BROUGHT THE BIRD BACK TO THE KICHEN, JEREMY LIKE
TO SNEAK PAST THE COOKS TO THE BASEMENT WHERE THE
WAITERS DRESSED FOR WORK. THERE HE WOULD BE ALONE,
AND HE COULD JUST SIT WITH THE DUCK. ITS WINGS WER
TIRED FROM BEATING AGAINST HIM, AND SOMETIMES IT
WOULD FALL ASLEEP ON HIS NECK.

ALL OF THE DUCKS WERE MALE, AND HAD BROWN AND BLUE FEATHERS. THEY WERE KILLED ON A WIPED-DOWN SURFACE IN THE MIDDLE OF THE KITCHEN. IT WAS A VERY HIGH-PAYING JOB. SOMETIMES THE COOK MADE A MISTAKE AND ORDERED A FEMALE, AND THEY WOULD SERVE IT AND SAY IT WAS A MALE. JEREMY DID NOT LIKE THE MAN WHO KILLED THE BIRDS WITH A KNIFE. WHEN THEY PASSED EACH OTHER IN THE HOT, NARROW PASSAGEWAYS OF THE KITCHEN, JEREMY SPIT ON THE FLOOR.

THE CUSTOMERS ALWAYS ASKED ABOUT COLOR OF THE FEATHERS, AND WHETHER IT WAS A BOY OR GIRL. THEY SMILED AND WERE HAPPY WHEN THEY COULD TASTE IT.

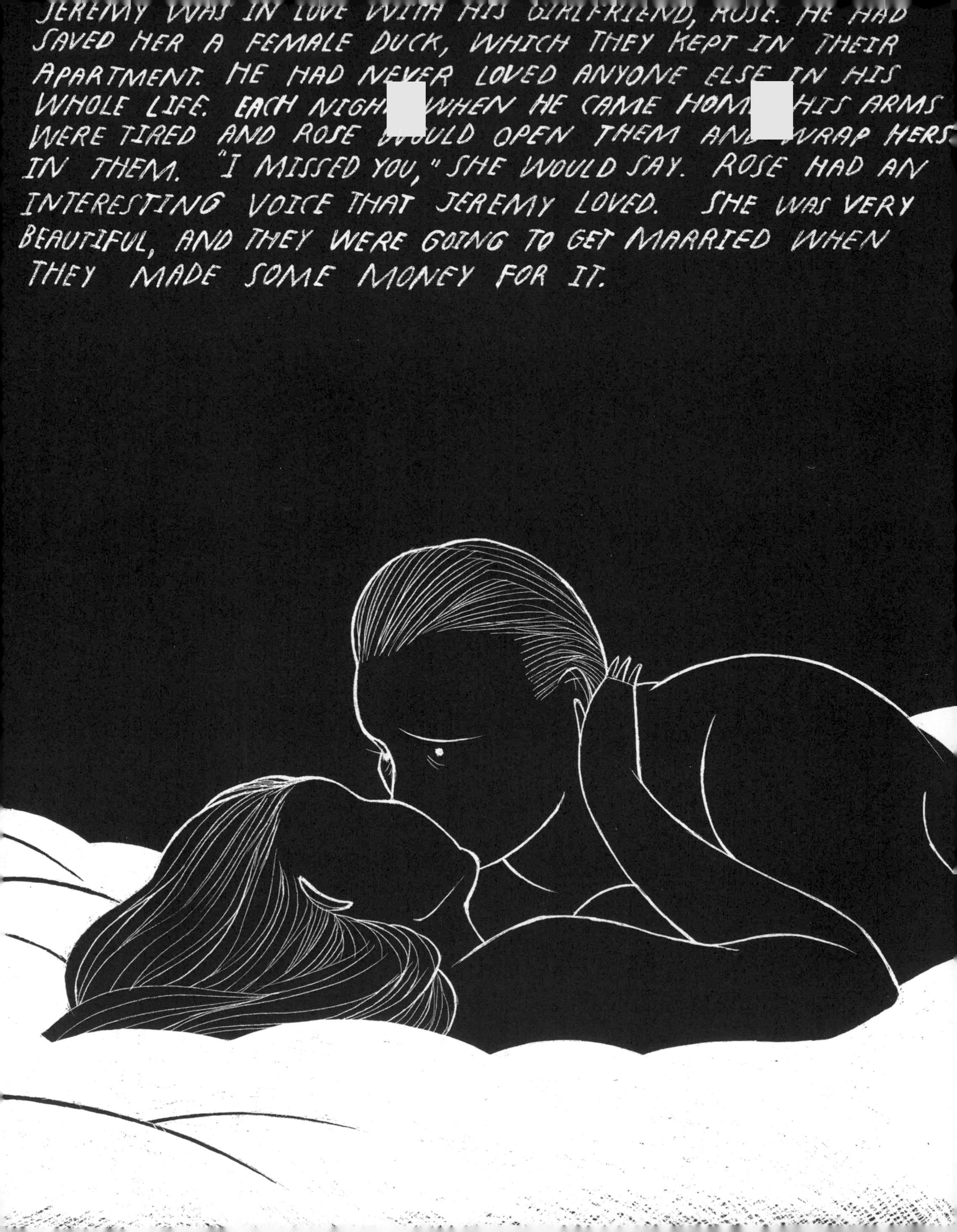
JEREMY WAS IN LOVE WITH HIS GIRLFRIEND, ROSE. HE HAD SAVED HER A FEMALE DUCK, WHICH THEY KEPT IN THEIR APARTMENT. HE HAD NEVER LOVED ANYONE ELSE IN HIS WHOLE LIFE. EACH NIGH[redacted] WHEN HE CAME HOM[redacted] HIS ARMS WERE TIRED AND ROSE [redacted]OULD OPEN THEM AND [redacted]WRAP HERS IN THEM. "I MISSED YOU," SHE WOULD SAY. ROSE HAD AN INTERESTING VOICE THAT JEREMY LOVED. SHE WAS VERY BEAUTIFUL, AND THEY WERE GOING TO GET MARRIED WHEN THEY MADE SOME MONEY FOR IT.

Rose thought about Jeremy working with the ducks every day, and how he sat with them in the basement.

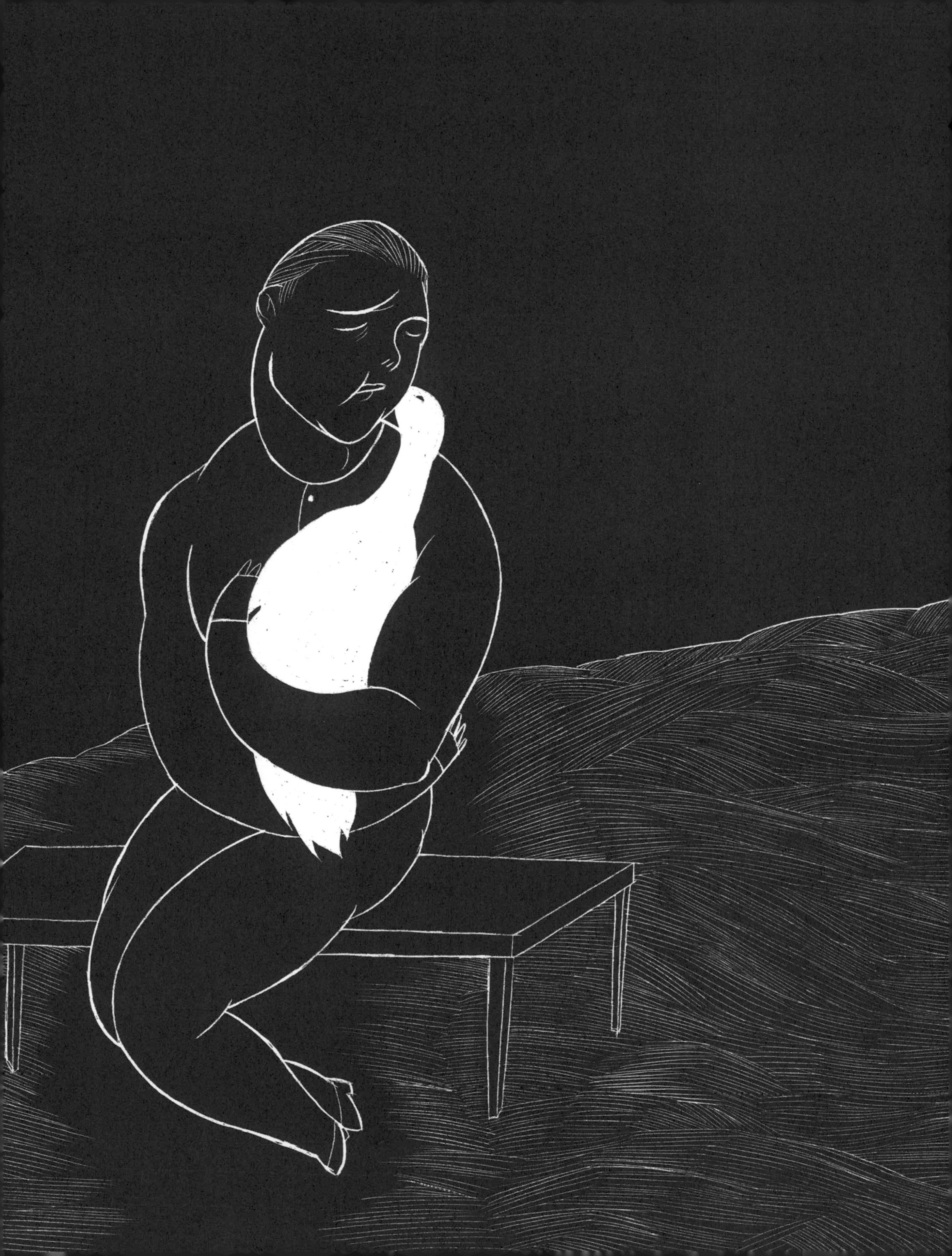

JEREMY AND ROSE WORKED UNTIL THEY HAD ENOUGH MONEY
TO GET MARRIED. THEIR WEDDING WAS INEXPENSIVE. THE
HEAD WAITER AT THE RESTAURANT CAME, AND ROSE'S MOTHER
AND FATHER, AND THAT WAS ALL. IT WAS IN A CHURCH
IN THE CITY WHERE THEY LIVED, AND AFTERWARD THEY
WENT HOME AND CRIED AND KISSED. THE NEXT DAY
JEREMY WENT BACK TO WORK.

ALL DAY LONG, JEREMY STOOD IN FRONT OF THE CUSTOMERS AND HELD THE DUCKS. "THIS ONE IS TOO THIN," THEY SAID. "THIS ONE IS NOT AS BROWN AS THE OTHERS," SAID OTHER CUSTOMERS.

WHEN HE CAME HOME THAT NIGHT, ROSE WAS IN BED. "MY THROAT
HURTS," SHE SAID. JEREMY STAYED UP ALL NIGHT HOLDING ONTO
HER BODY WITH HIS BIG ARMS, THE DUCK ASLEEP AGAINST
THEM.

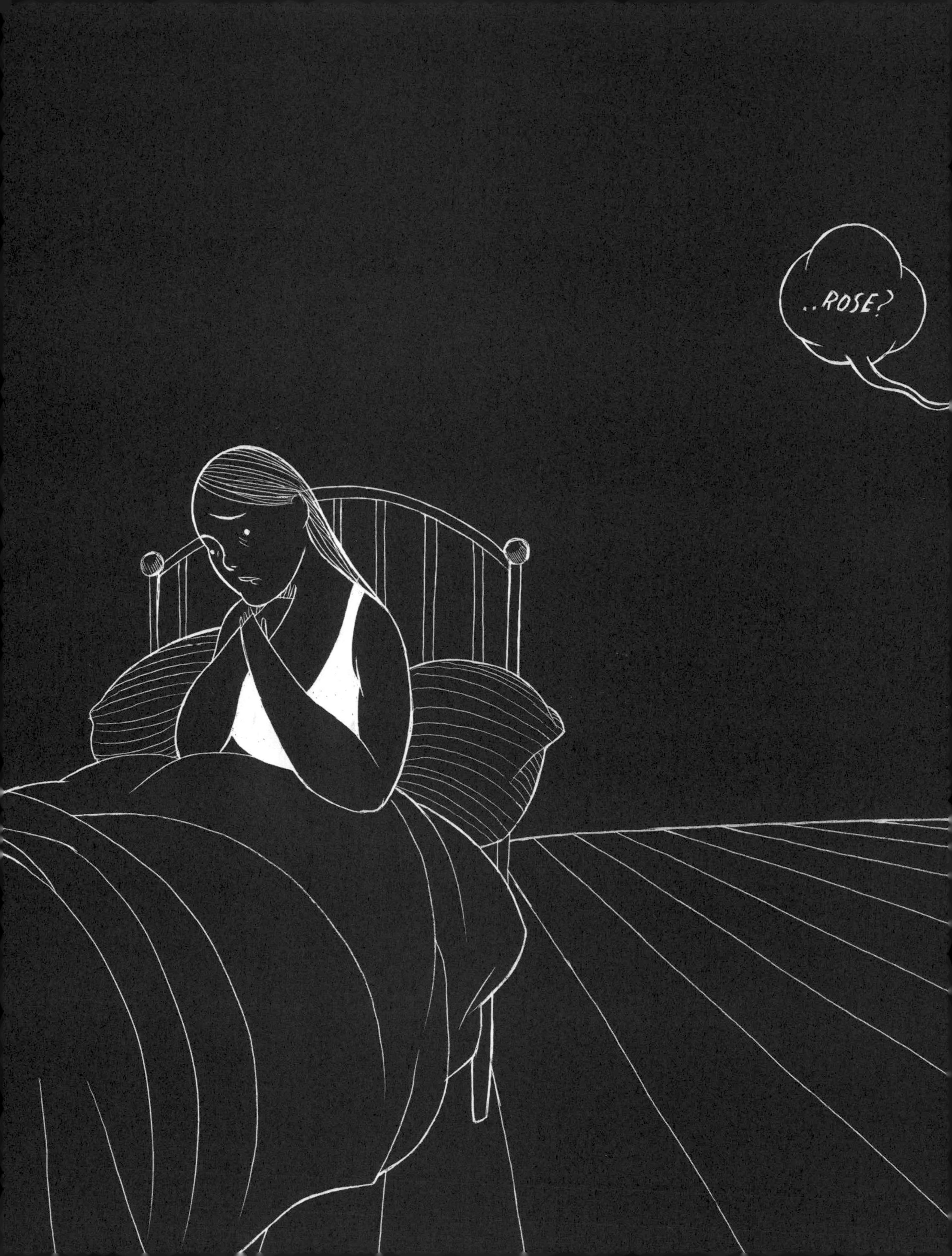
..ROSE?

BY THE MORNING, ROSE HAD GOTTEN BAD. HER THROAT WAS
SWOLLEN AND SHE COULD NOT SPEAK. JEREMY CALLED THE
DOCTOR AND THEY CAME AND TOOK HER TO THE HOSPITAL.
HE WAITED FOR A VERY LONG TIME IN THE WAITING
ROOM, STANDING UP AND SITTING BACK DOWN AGAIN.
"SHE IS VERY SICK," SAID THE DOCTOR WHEN HE CAME OUT,
"HER THROAT IS CLOSED UP AND SHE WILL DIE." JEREMY
KNEW HIS LIFE WAS GONE. THEY MADE A PLACE
FOR HIM TO SLEEP IN THE ROOM WITH ROSE, NEXT TO
HER HEAD. HE TOOK HER INTO HIS ARMS AND CRIED
ON TOP OF HER. HE CRIED AND CRIED.

Rose stayed asleep with her throat closed. She could not speak or hear. She slept in the hospital and Jeremy slept next to her every night. "We will put her someplace safe until the end," said the doctors. "You should go home." Jeremy had forgotten to sleep or eat.

WHEN HE GOT HOME, JEREMY LOOKED AT THE EMPTY APARTMENT AND THE SPACE ON THE BED WHERE ROSE'S BODY HAD BEEN. HE FELT VERY SICK. THE DUCK WAS THERE, ASLEEP ON THE PILLOW. HIS ARMS BECAME HARD AND HE TOOK THE DUCK FROM THE BED AND BROUGHT IT TO THE KITCHEN. HE FOUND A FORK AND KNIFE AND STUCK THE FORK INTO IT'S THROAT. THE DUCK FLAPPED AND BEAT SILENTLY AGAINST THE TABLE. JEREMY LET IT JERK AND THUMP, AND THEN HE PUT THE KNIFE INTO IT'S BREAST AND TURNED IT. HE DID NOT FEEL SICK ANYMORE. FEATHERS STUCK TO HIS CHEST WITH SWEAT AND BLOOD. HE CUT THE DUCK'S HEAD OFF AND PUT IT'S BODY IN A BOWL AND WENT TO SLEEP.

WHEN HE WENT BACK TO THE RESTAURANT, JEREMY DID NOT
SPEAK TO ANYONE. AFTER A WHILE, HE ASKED IF HE COULD
TAKE THE JOB OF KILLING THE DUCKS. "OK," SAID THE
HEAD COOK. JEREMY'S SHOULDERS WERE HEAVY.

JEREMY KILLED THE BIRDS FASTER AND HARDER, UNTIL HE
BECAME THE BEST BUTCHER THE RESTAURANT HAD EVER SEEN.
HE KILLED MORE DUCKS THAN THE COOK COULD BOIL. HIS ARMS
WERE STEADY AND HARD IN THE DULL LIGHT OF THE KITCHEN.
HE DID NOT SPEAK EXCEPT TO ASK FOR THE NEXT ONE.
EVERYNIGHT WHEN HE CAME HOME, JEREMY SAT ON THE BED
AND PICKED FEATHERS OFF HIS CHEST AND NECK. HE DID
NOT VISIT ROSE ANYMORE.

THE RESTAURANT BECAME EVEN MORE FAMOUS OVER THE YEARS,
AND JEREMY KILLED MORE AND MORE BIRDS. ALL OF THE
WAITERS STAYED FAR AWAY FROM HIM IN THE HALLS,
AND SPIT ON THE FLOOR WHEN HE PASSED.

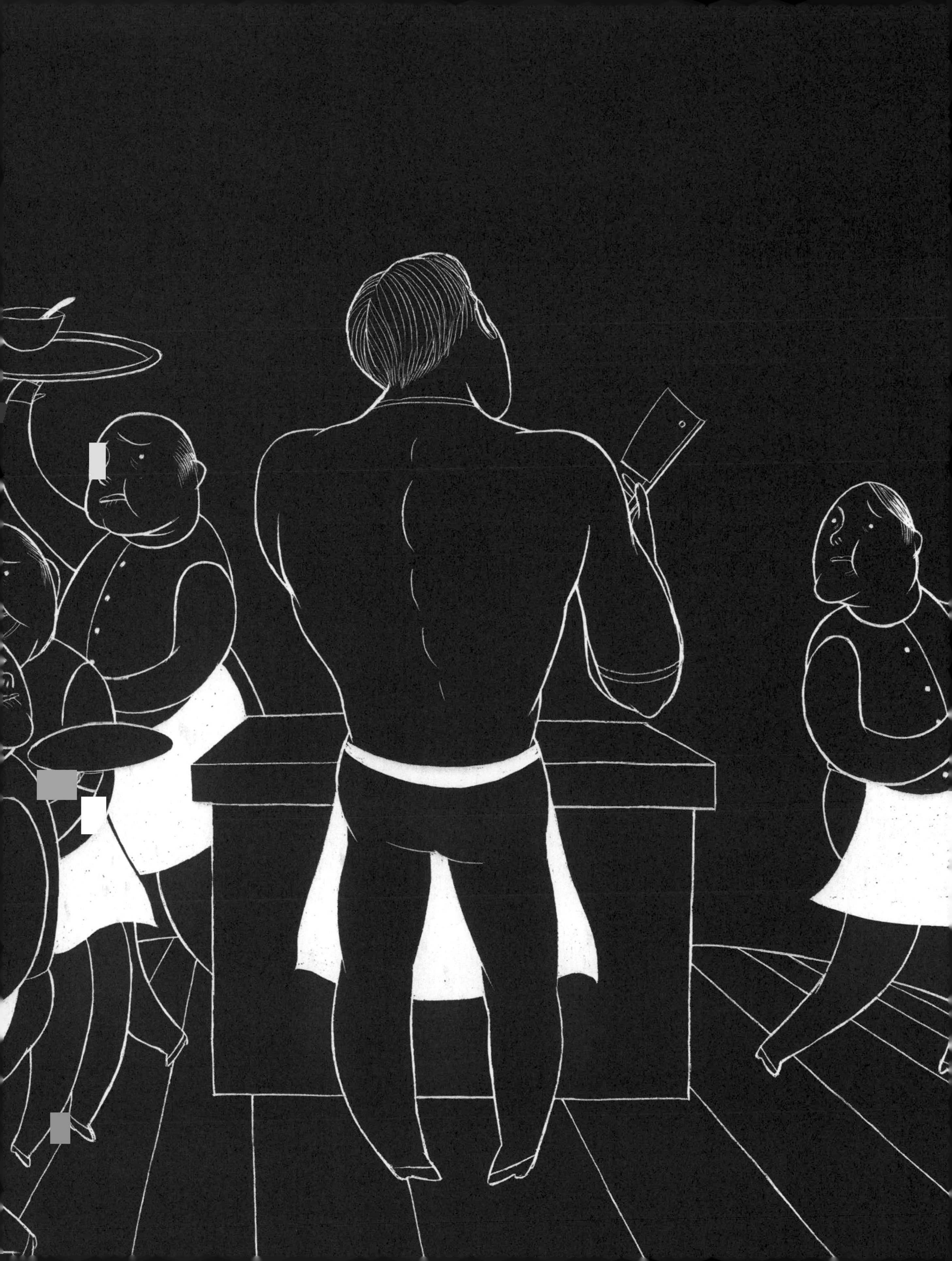

THEN ONE DAY, SOMETHING HAPPENED. THE DOCTOR CALLED AND SAID THAT ROSE HAD GOTTEN BETTER. "IT IS A MIRACLE," HE SAID. JEREMY NOTICED THAT THE DOCTOR WAS CRYING. "YOU CAN PICK HER UP NOW." JEREMY THOUGHT ABOUT THE PET DUCK THAT HE KILLED. THEN HE THOUGHT OF THE HUNDREDS OF DUCKS HE HAD KILLED AFTER THAT. HE DID NOT PICK HER UP.

THE NEXT DAY, JEREMY WENT TO WORK. HE KILLED MANY, MANY BIRDS. HE STUCK THE FORK INTO THEIR NECKS, AND WHEN THEY MOVED, HE STUCK IT INTO THEIR EYES. HE WORKED VERY HARD ALL DAY. WHEN THE HOSPITAL CALLED, HE DID NOT ANSWER. HE WENT HOME THAT NIGHT AND CLEANED HIS SHIRT IN THE SINK AND WENT TO BED. HE DID THE SAME THING THE NEXT DAY, AND THE NEXT. AFTER A WHILE, THE HOSPITAL STOPPED CALLING.

MANY MONTHS LATER, CUSTOMERS WHO HAD KNOWN ROSE SAID THAT THEY HAD SEEN HER LOOKING INTO THE WINDOWS OF THE RESTAURANT. SHE WOULD STAND, WITH WET AND RED EYES, FOR A VERY LONG TIME. SOMETIMES SHE WOULD GO INSIDE AND STAND IN THE BACK OF THE ROOM UNTIL THEY ASKED HER TO LEAVE. SHE DID THIS FOR A WHILE AND THEN STOPPED, EVENTUALLY.

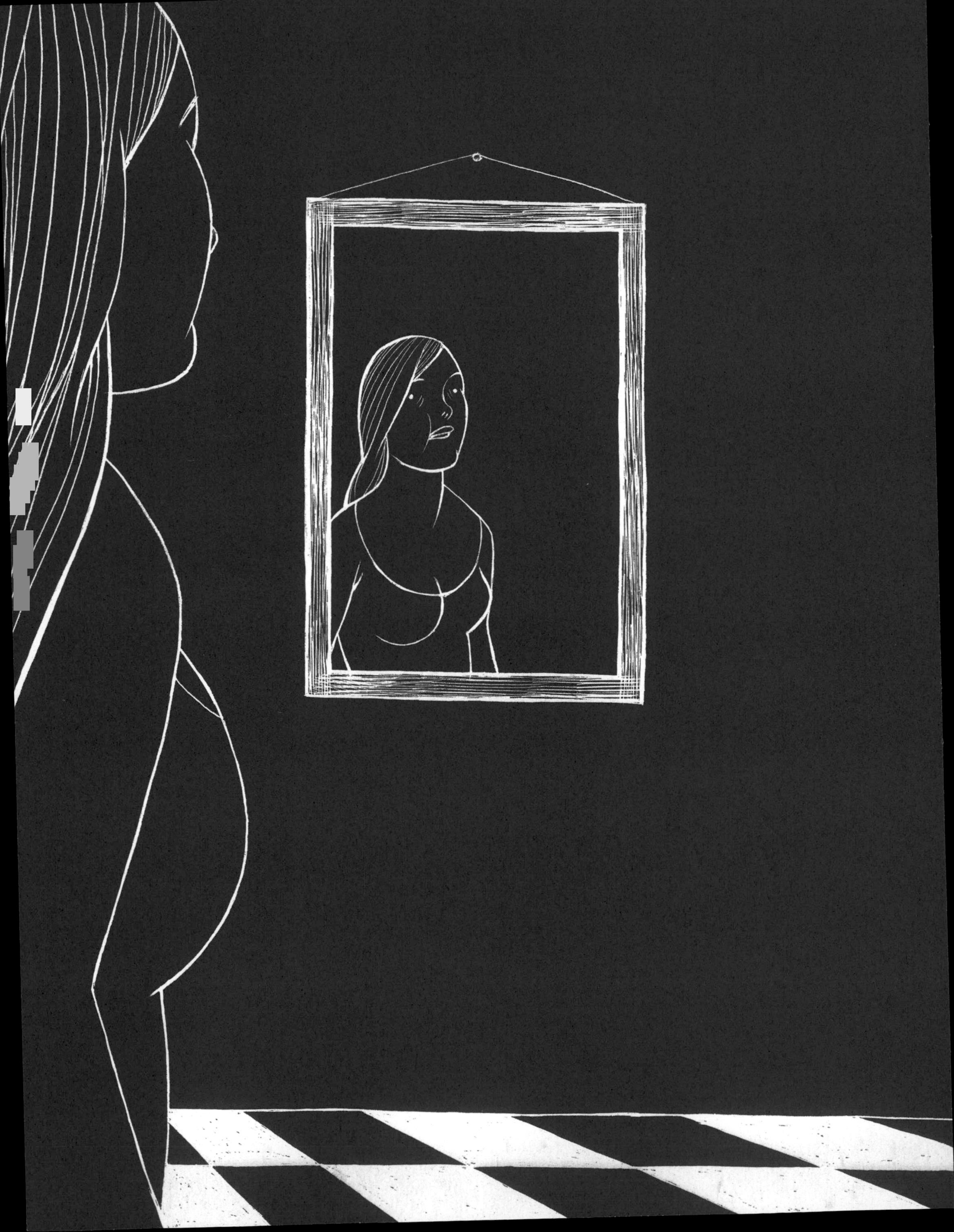

THE END

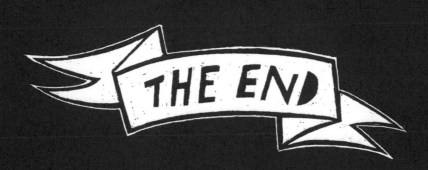

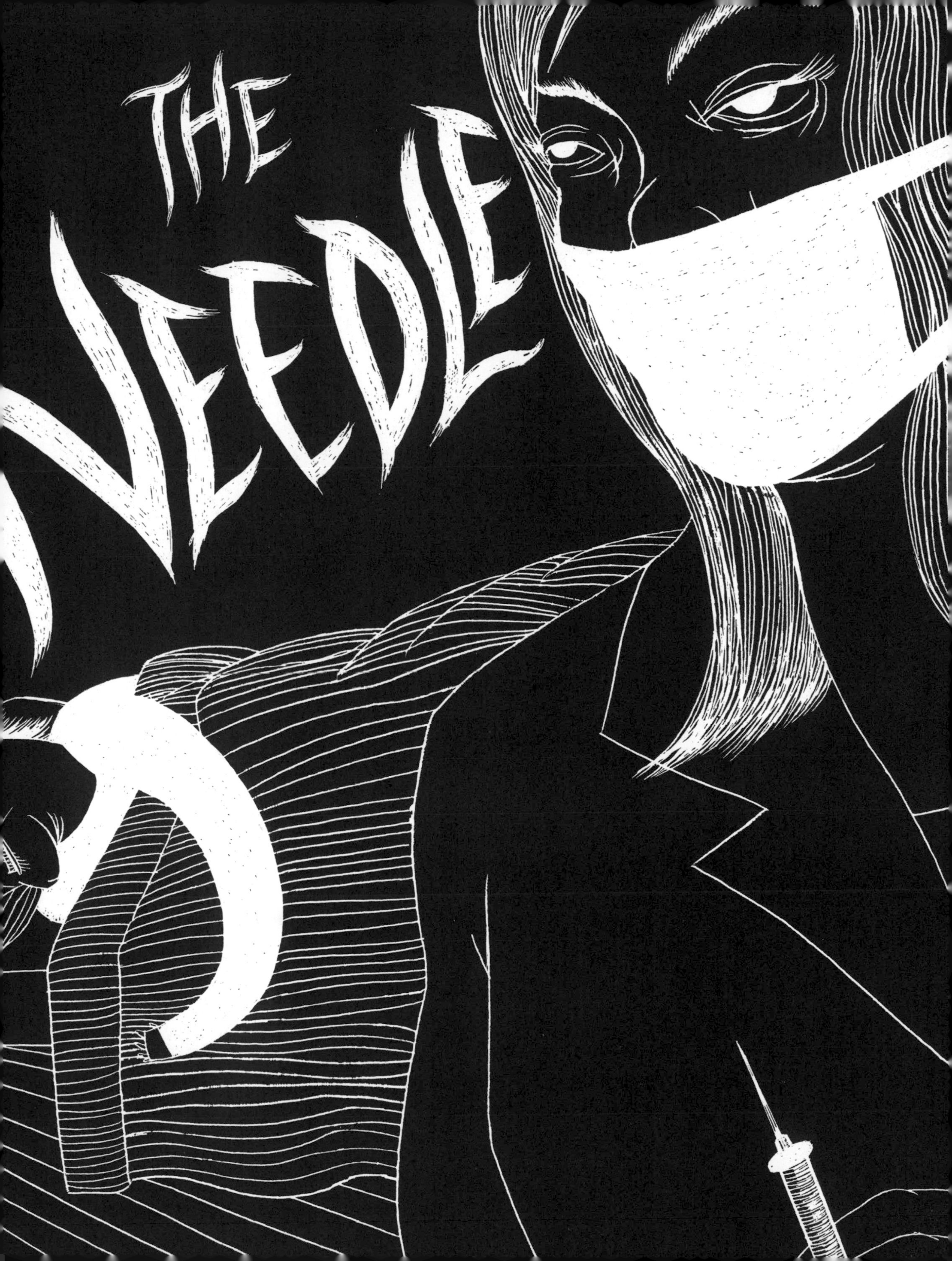
THE NEEDLE

THE CHILDREN HAD GOTTEN TO HER BEFORE SHE WAS DEAD, BUT IT WAS VERY TIGHT. THEY HAD BEEN ON AN ISLAND WITH THEIR FATHER. WHEN THEY ARRIVED, IT WAS EVENING.

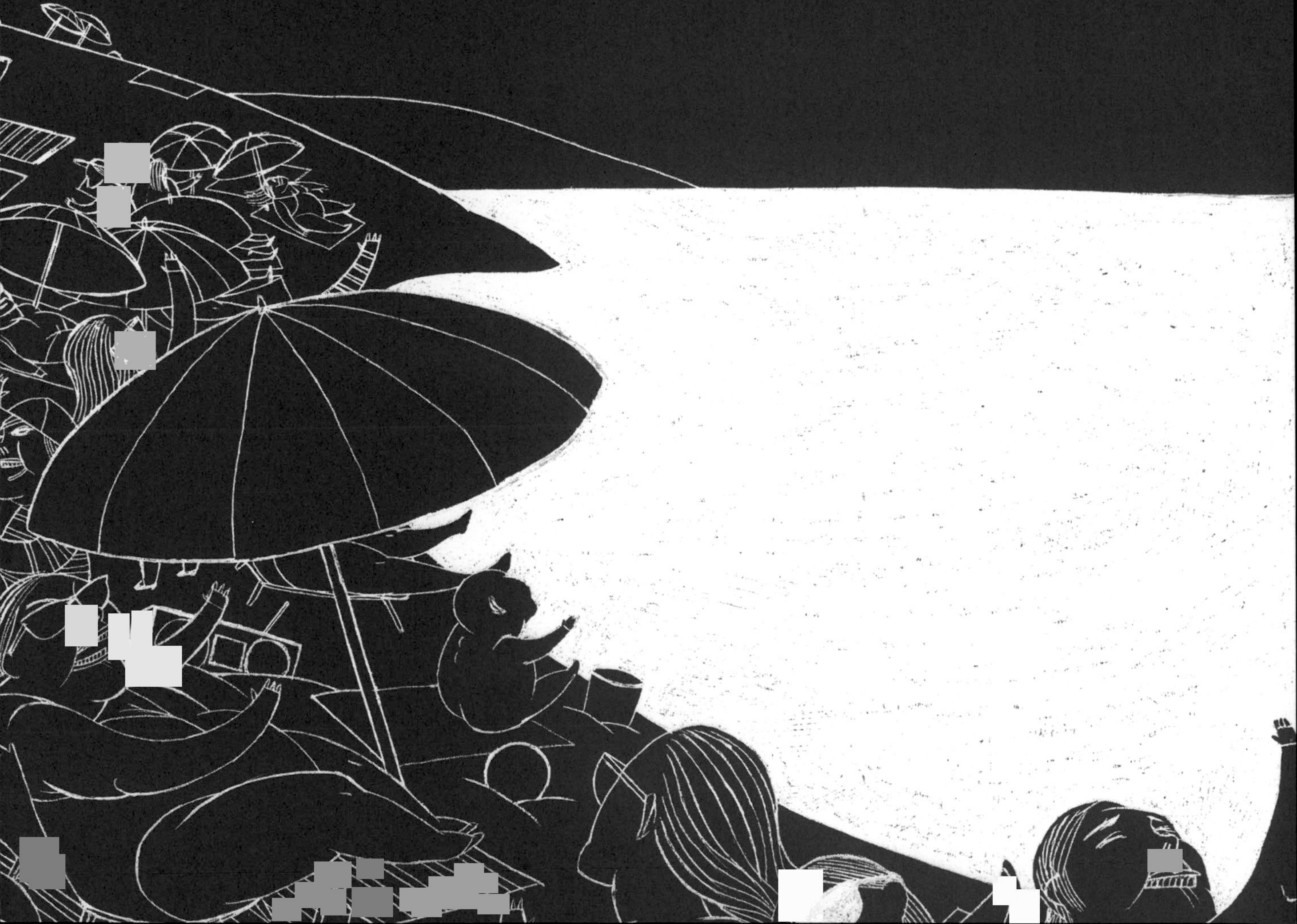

SHE WAS VERY OLD, BUT HAD SUSTAINED OLD AGE WITHOUT DYING
FOR SOME TIME. THE CHILDREN HAD NOT SEEN DEATH BEFORE,
AND WHEN THEY CAME INTO HER ROOM, THEY BURST INTO
TEARS. SHE WAS THEIR MOTHER'S MOTHER, AND HAD
LARGE HANDS THAT WERE ALREADY STARTING TO POKE THROUGH
THEIR DREAMS AT NIGHT, AND WOULD CONTINUE TO DO SO FOR
THE REST OF THEIR LIVES.
THERE WAS ANOTHER WOMAN IN THE ROOM AS WELL, STANDING
TOLERANTLY IN THE CORNER WITH A NEEDLE.

BOTH OF THE CHILDREN WERE GIRLS. THEY WERE TEENAGERS, AND IN THE PROCESS OF BEING IN LOVE SERIOUSLY FOR THE FIRST TIME, SO AFTER THEY CRIED INTO HER CHEST AND HANDS, THEY WENT AND CRIED INTO THE PHONE. THEN THEY CAME BACK TO WATCH HER BREATHE SOME MORE. SHE WAS BIG AND WARM, AND PANTING. AT NIGHT, THE MOTHER AND THE CHILDREN SAT CLOSE TO HER MOUTH UNTIL THEY HAD TO GO TO BED. THE CHILDRENS BOYFRIENDS CAME AS WELL, AND THEY CRIED INTO THEM AND KISSED AND FELT THE PLEASURE OF A NEW KIND OF SADNESS.

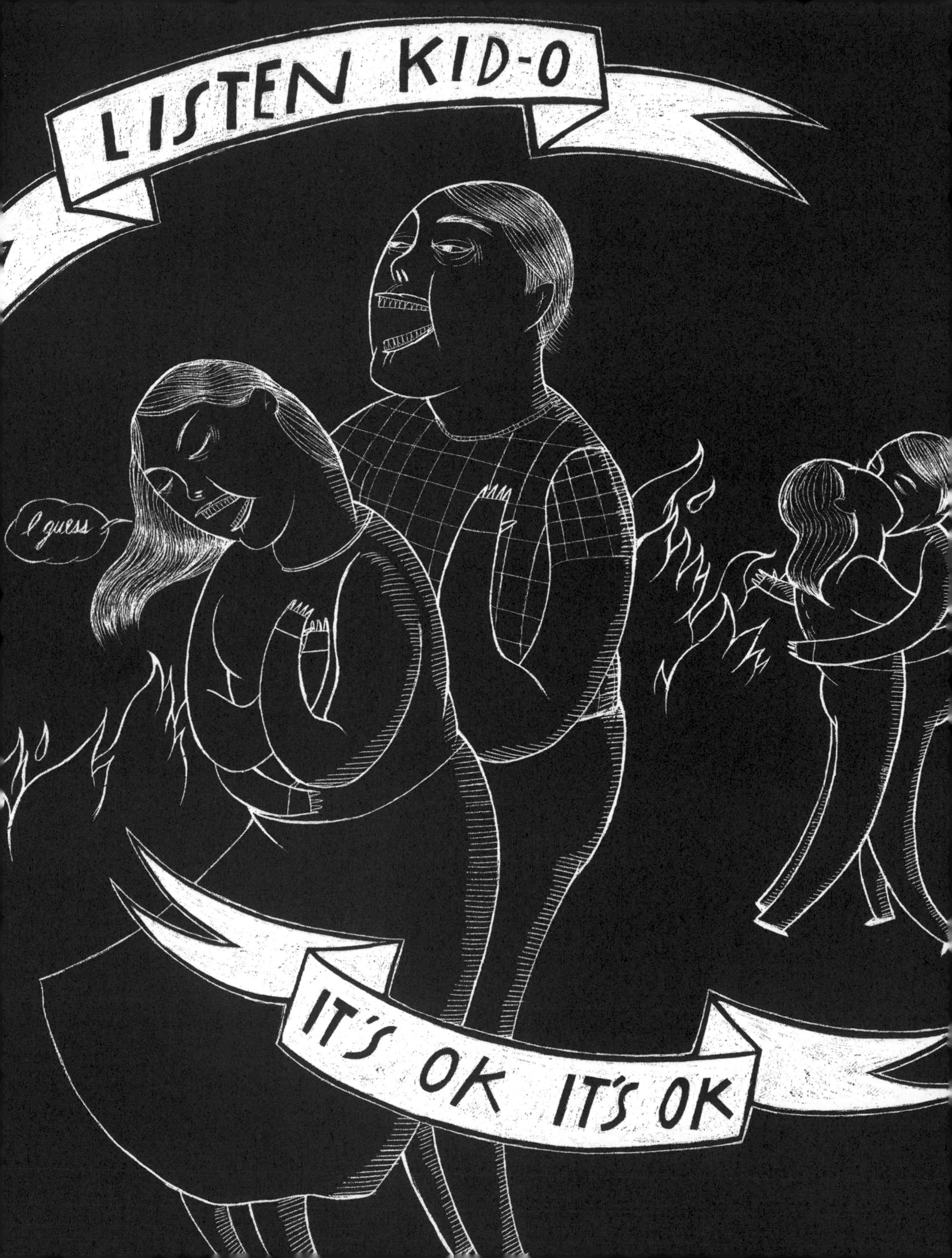
LISTEN KID-O
I guess
IT'S OK IT'S OK

THE NEXT MORNING, THE CHILDREN WOKE UP LATE AND FOUND OUT THAT THEIR GRANDMOTHER HAD DIED WHILE THEY WERE IN THE SHOWER. THE MOTHER CRIED VERY HARD, AND THE CHILDREN WERE RELIEVED THAT THEY DID NOT SEE IT HAPPEN, AS IT WOULD HAVE BEEN GLOOMY AND STRAIGHTFORWARD. THEY LATER FOUND OUT THAT THE WOMAN WITH THE NEEDLE HAD GIVEN HER A FINAL SHOT.

THE REST OF THE DAY THE CHILDREN HELPED THEIR MOTHER FIND THINGS TO PUT AWAY, AND TAKE OUT, AND PUT AWAY AGAIN.

THE WOMAN WITH THE NEEDLE STAYED ALL DAY IN THE HOUSE
WITH THEM, THOUGH NO ONE WAS SURE WHY. SHE WAS
A BLONDE WOMAN WITH BRIGHT EYES AND MINT-COLORED
PANTS. THE CHILDREN DID NOT GO UPSTAIRS TO SEE THE LADY
FOR THE WHOLE DAY. WHEN THEY FINALLY WENT INTO THE
BEDROOM, THEY **LOOKED** AT THE CORPSE AND KNEW THAT THEY
WERE SEEING SOMETHING VERY SPECIAL.

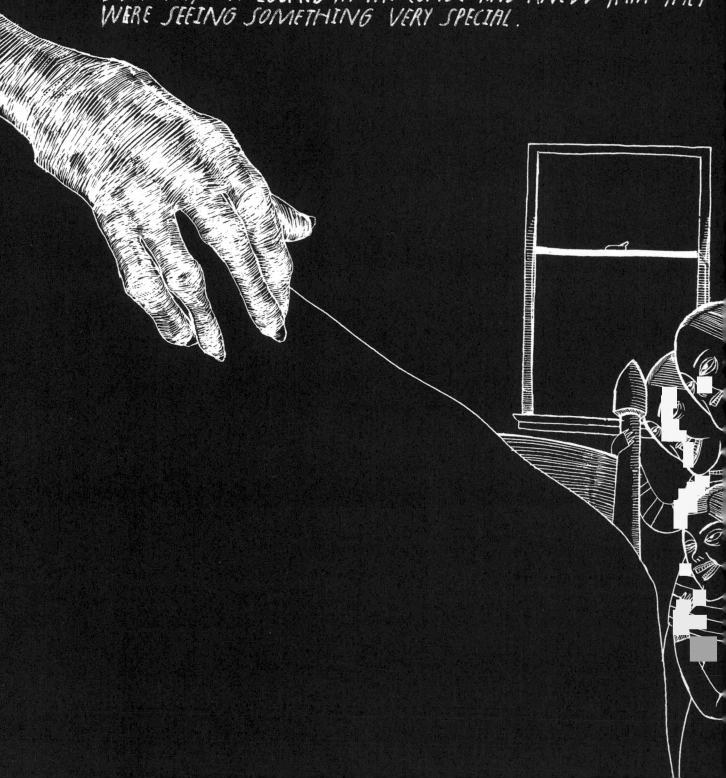

AFTER THE FUNERAL THE NEXT DAY, THE CHILDREN CLASPED EACH OTHER'S HANDS TIGHTLY IN THE CAR AS THEIR MOTHER DROVE HOME. THEY PASSED THE WOMAN WITH THE NEEDLE ON THE HIGHWAY. SHE WAS DRIVING ALONGSIDE THEM IN A SMALL CAR.

SHE STILL HAD ON THE MINT PANTS, AND THE CHILDREN COULD SEE THROUGH THE WINDOW THAT SHE WAS SINGING ALONG TO A SONG WITH UNCANNY JOY. HER HANDS WERE CLEAN AND DANCED ACROSS THE STEERING WHEEL BUT DID NOT GIVE OFF THE EFFECT OF TAPPING IN RHYTHM. INSTEAD, THEY SPRUNG OVER HER HAIR, HER OWN LIPS, AND BACK ONTO THE LEATHER OF THE WHEEL AS IF SHE WERE REENACTING THE THRILL OF AN EXOTIC SENSATION THAT HAD BEEN CARRIED OUT IN A PLACE FAR FROM WHERE SHE WAS NOW. THE SILENT MUSIC SEEMED ROWDY, AND THE CHILDREN NOTICED HER MOUTH THE SAME WORDS OVER AND OVER SEVERAL TIMES IN A ROW, WHICH WAS WHAT THEY UNDERSTOOD TO BE THE CHORUS.

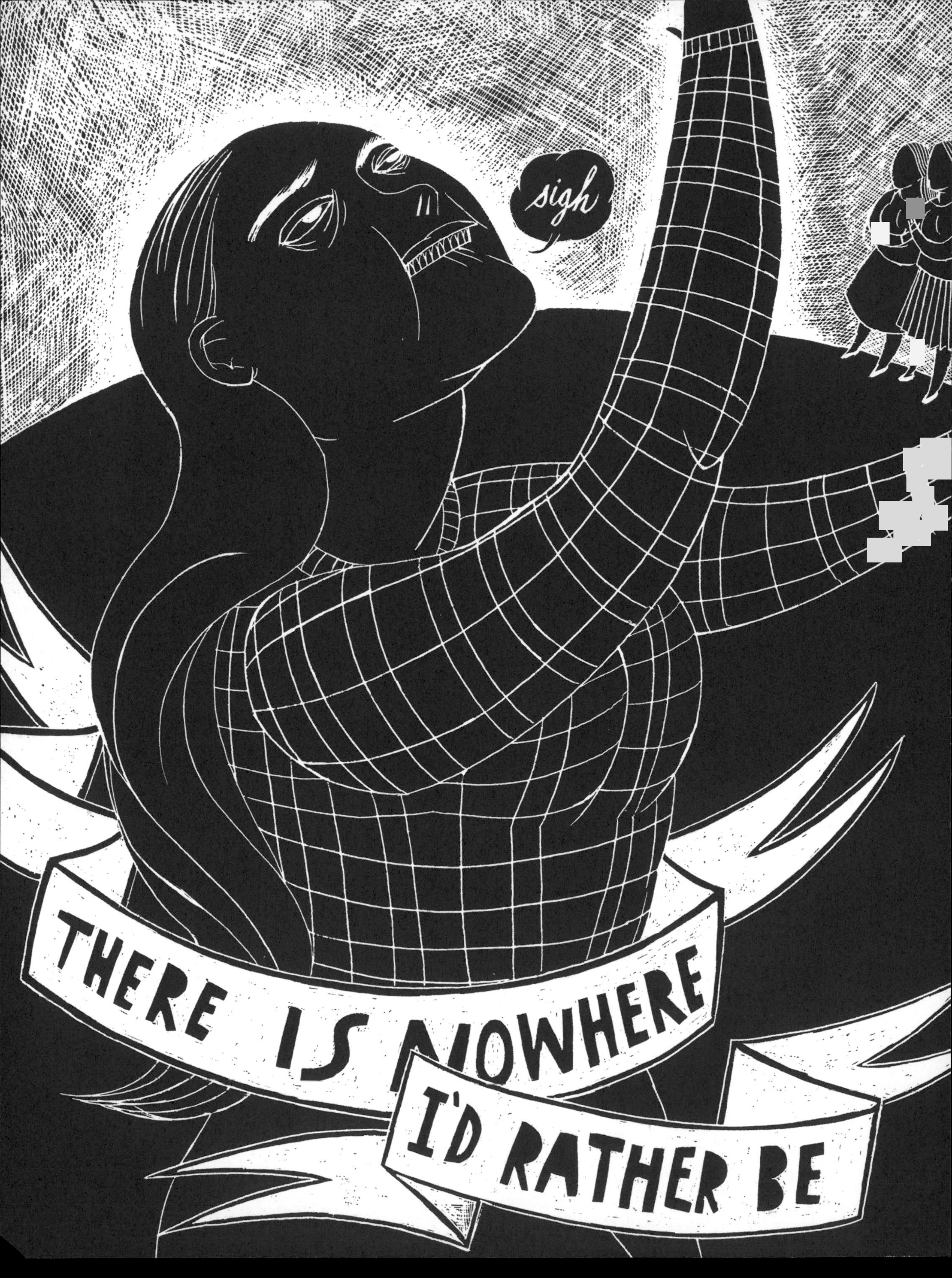
sigh
THERE IS NOWHERE
I'D RATHER BE

SOME YEARS LATER, THE CHILDREN WERE MID-ATLANTIC ON A
TREMENDOUS OCEAN-LINER. THEY WERE WITH THEIR MOTHER
ON THEIR WAY TO AN EXPENSIVE VACATION IN GREECE. THE
CHILDREN HAD GROWN INTO YOUNG ADULTS AND HAD BEAUTIFUL
THINGS TO SAY ABOUT EVERYTHING. ON THE THIRD-TO-LAST
DAY OF SAILING, THEY SAW THE WOMAN WITH THE NEEDLE.

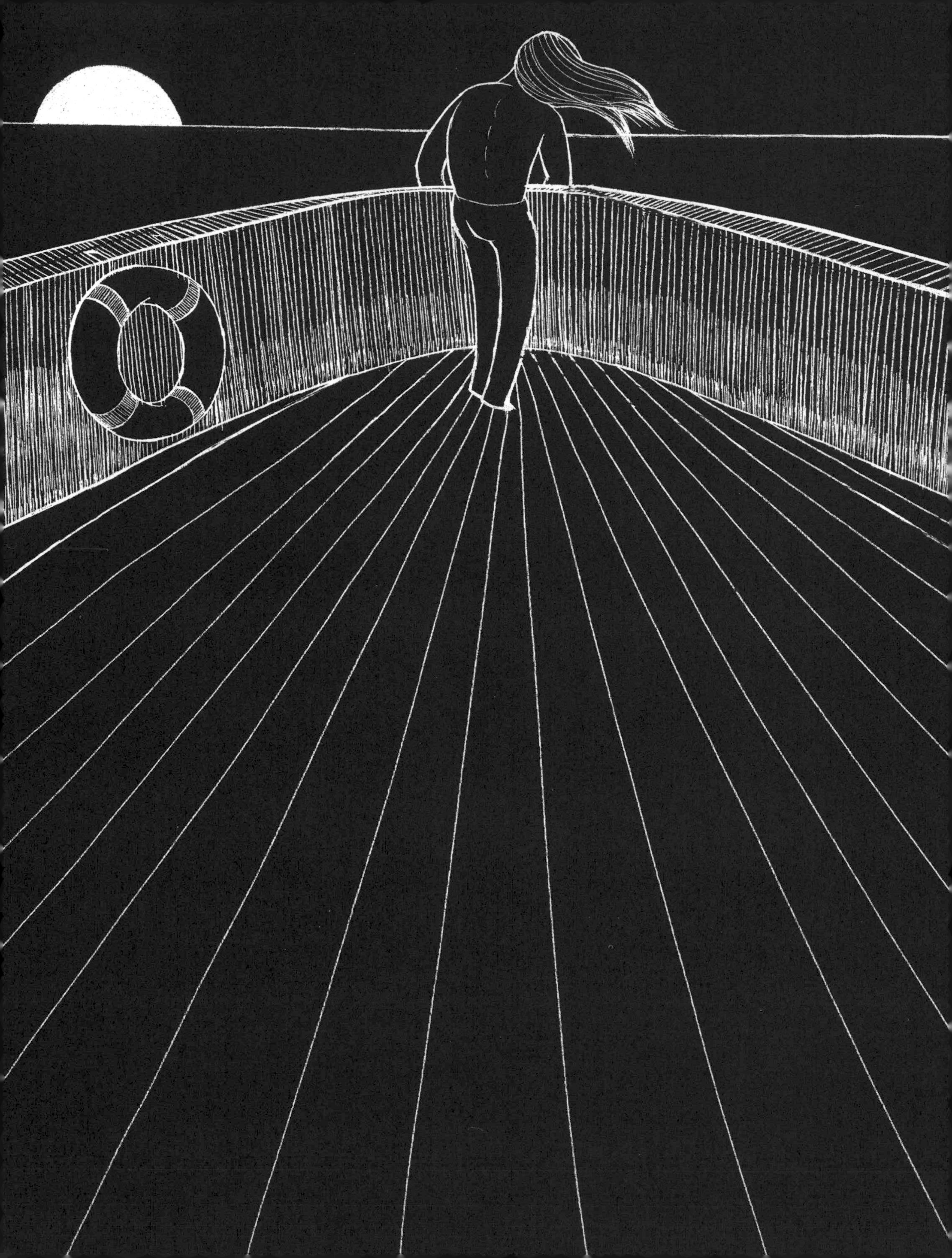

SHE WAS STANDING ON THE HIGH DECK OF THE BOW, CRANING HER NECK DOWNWARD TO LOOK AT SOME SEALS THAT WERE THROWING THEMSELVES VIOLENTLY IN AND OUT OF THE WAKE OF THE SHIP. THE DARK, OILY ANIMALS SEEMED TO GIVE HER PLEASURE, AND SHE SMILED AND MOVED BACK-AND-FORTH WITH THE ACTION OF THE WAVES.

THE CHILDREN WERE ALARMED AT SEEING HER THERE. THEY ALSO DID NOT WANT TO UPSET THEIR MOTHER. THEY MANAGED TO DISTRACT HER BEFORE SHE SAW THE WOMAN WITH THE NEEDLE BY PUSHING THEMSELVES INTO A BALLROOM THAT WAS OFF OF THE PROMENADE DECK. A HEAVE OF GREEK CONGA-LINE DANCERS ENVELOPED THEM, AND NO ONE SAW THE WOMAN FOR THE REST OF THE TRIP. THE CHILDREN, HOWEVER, HAD PERSISTENT DREAMS ABOUT THINGS BEING BROUGHT BACK TO LIFE, AND BECAME FATIGUED AND DISORIENTED DURING THE AFTERNOONS WITH NO EXPLANATION.

THEY SAW THE WOMAN AGAIN, HALF A YEAR LATER, ON A WET
EVENING IN THE CITY. SHE WAS COMING OUT OF AN APARTMENT
THAT WAS CLOSE TO WHERE THE CHILDREN LIVED. THE WOMAN
WITH THE NEEDLE WORE A SIMILAR SHADE OF PANTS, AND
THE SAME LIGHT SKIN. HER HANDS WERE SMACKING UP
AND DOWN AGAINST HER THIGHS AS SHE WALKED. SHE
DID NOT SEEM TO NOTICE ANYONE AROUND HER.
SHE WALKED TO THE CORNER WHERE HER CAR WAS AND REMOVED
A GLOSSY DOCTOR'S BAG FROM THE FRONT SEAT AND PUT IT IN
THE TRUNK. THE CHILDREN WATCHED THE CAR PUSH INTO THE
STREET AND DRIVE AWAY. IT WAS NIGHT, AND THE LOW,
OPTIMISTIC SOUND OF SIRENS ON THEIR WAY TO HOSPITALS
REVIVED THE AIR.

THEY SAW THE WOMAN SIX MORE TIMES BY THE END OF THAT
YEAR.

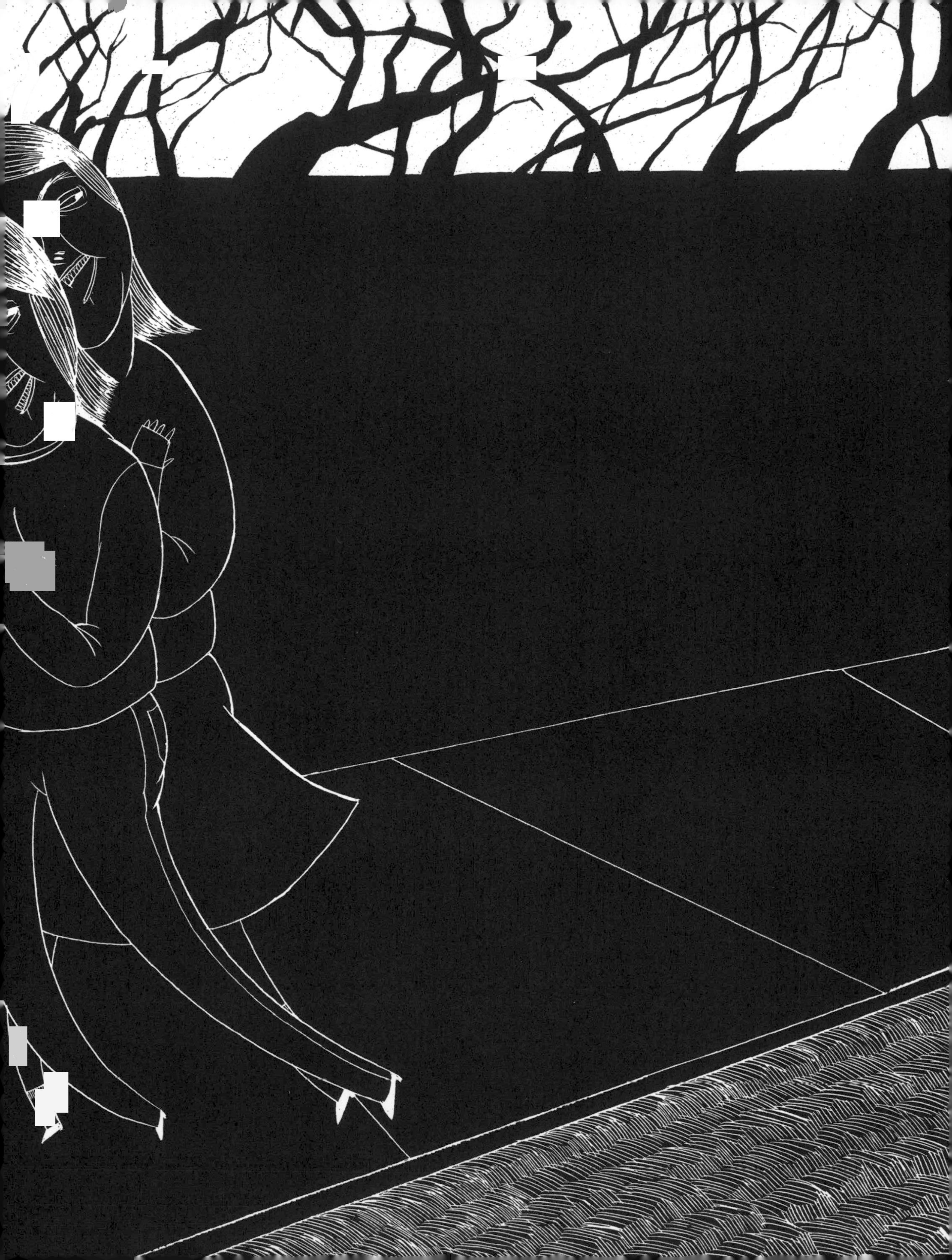

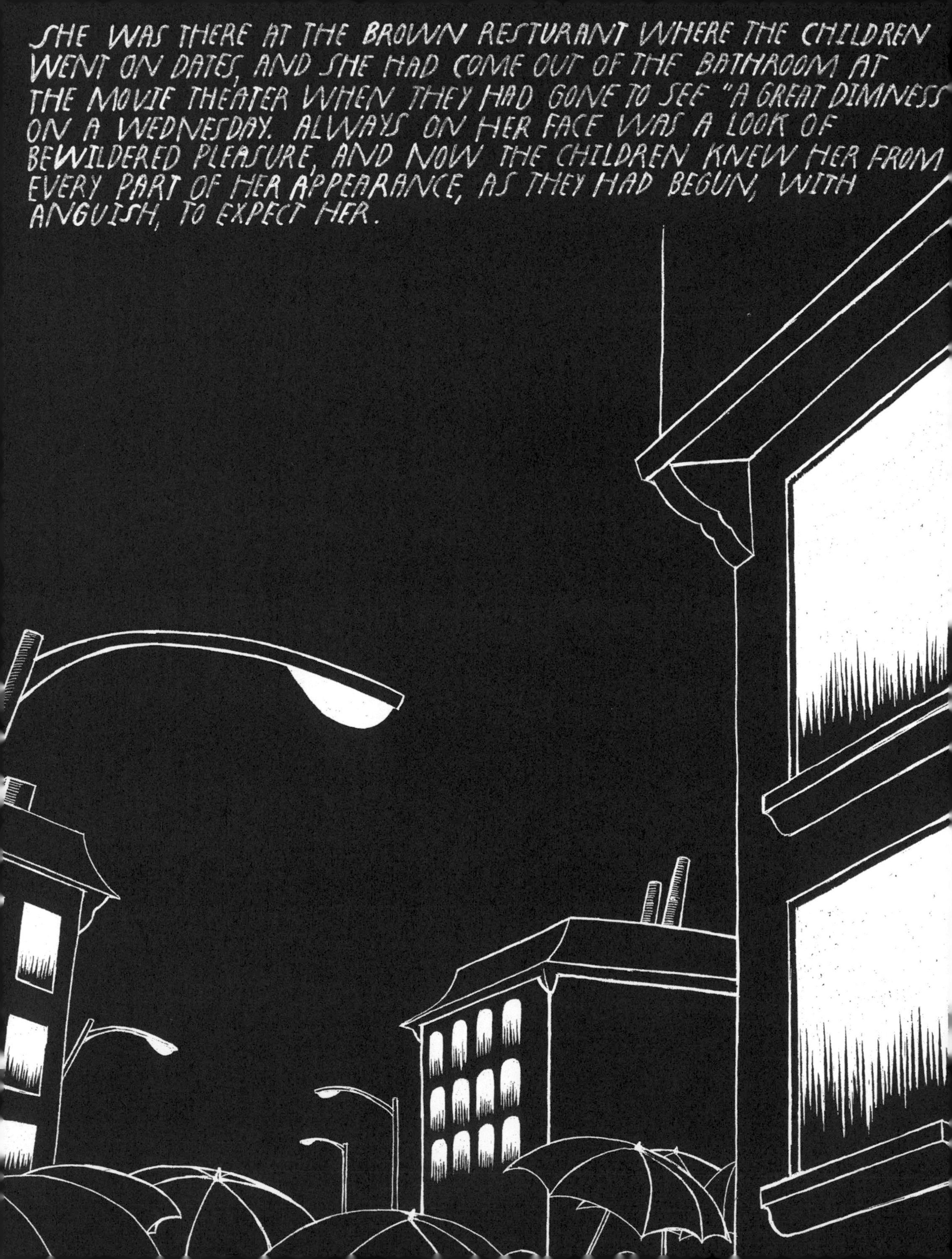
SHE WAS THERE AT THE BROWN RESTURANT WHERE THE CHILDREN WENT ON DATES, AND SHE HAD COME OUT OF THE BATHROOM AT THE MOVIE THEATER WHEN THEY HAD GONE TO SEE "A GREAT DIMNESS" ON A WEDNESDAY. ALWAYS ON HER FACE WAS A LOOK OF BEWILDERED PLEASURE, AND NOW THE CHILDREN KNEW HER FROM EVERY PART OF HER APPEARANCE, AS THEY HAD BEGUN, WITH ANGUISH, TO EXPECT HER.

ONE DAY THERE WAS A RAIN THAT FELL CONSTANTLY, AND THE
CHILDREN HAD TO RUSH TO AND FROM THE SUBWAY IN ORDER
TO GET PLACES. ON A STREET NEAR THEIR FRONT DOOR, THEY
SAW THE WOMAN. SHE WAS COMING OUT OF A STORE CALLED
"FANCY IMPORTS," DRAGGING SOMETHING HEAVY NEXT
TO HER LIKE A DARK, SIGNIFICANT PIECE OF FURNITURE. HER
SMILE WAS CUT WITH CONCENTRATION, WHICH THE CHILDREN
HAD NEVER SEEN BEFORE.
THE BIG THING THAT THE WOMAN WAS PUSHING HAD ON A
JACKET, OR SOMETHING WET, FLAPPING IN THE RAIN. THE
WOMAN DID NOT HAVE AN UMBRELLA. SHE WAS HOOKED
TO THE THING WITH ONE ARM, AND HAD THE DOCTOR'S
BAG ON THE OTHER. THEY PUSHED TOGETHER INTO THE PARKING
LOT AND THE WOMAN LOOKED UP SO THAT BIG DRIPS HIT
HER IN THE EYES AND SHE SHUDDERED. WHEN SHE WAS
ALMOST AT HER CAR, THE CHILDREN COULD SEE THE DRESSING
GOWN OF THE THING SHE WAS CONNECTED TO. IT TURNED
IT'S FACE AROUND SLOWLY, AND LOOKED AT THEM WITH SOAKED,
POLITE EYES. THE CHILDREN REALIZED IT WAS THEIR GRANDMOTHER,
AND THE WOMAN WITH THE NEEDLE CLOSED THE DOOR
AND THEY DROVE OFF.

SINCE THEY HAD BOTH SEEN IT, THE CHILDREN DECIDED IT WAS REAL. WHEN THEY CALLED THEIR MOTHER, SHE WEPT AND TOLD THEM IT WAS NOT REAL. THE CHILDREN WENT BACK TO HAVING DREAMS ABOUT RESURRECTION, AND A CORPSE WITH GREAT SOFT HANDS, AND OTHER TIMES IT WOULD NOT BE A PERSON AT ALL, BUT A GROWN-UP ANIMAL.

EVENTUALLY THEY DID NOT DREAM AT ALL. THEY LEFT THEIR APARTMENTS EVERY MORNING WITH A MISTY SENSE OF HORROR, AND DID NOT SEE THEIR BOYFRIENDS ANYMORE. INSTEAD, THEY SPENT LONG NIGHTS TOGETHER, LOOKING UP AND DOWN THE STAIRCASES IN THEIR BUILDING. THEY DID NOT SEE THE WOMAN AGAIN. MANY YEARS PASSED.

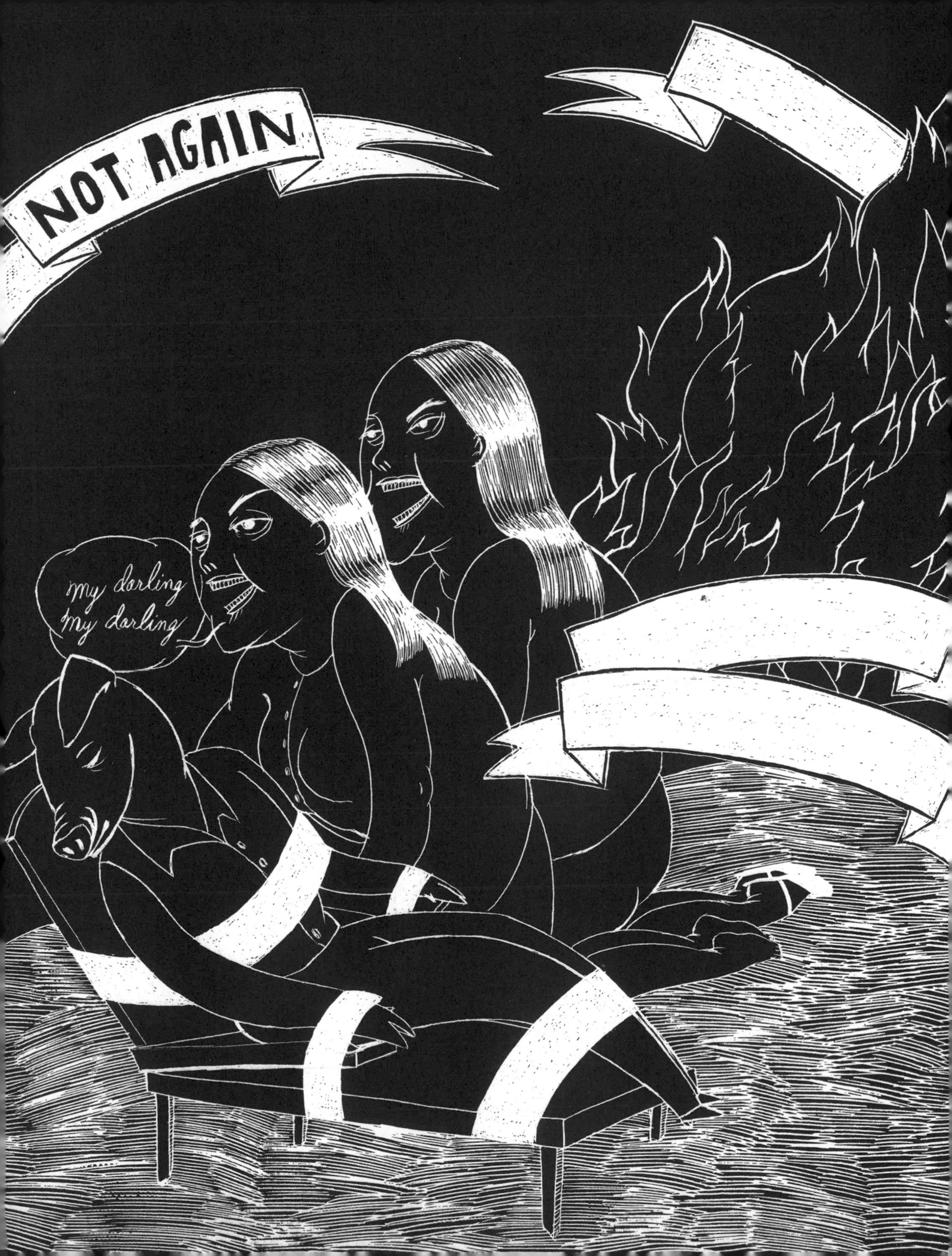
NOT AGAIN
my darling
my darling

WHEN A LONG-TIME FAMILY NEIGHBOR DIED OF AN INFLAMED HEART, THE CHILDREN WERE SUMMONED FOR THE FUNERAL. THE SERVICE WAS LIKE A GRADUATION, WITH MUSIC AND READING, AND THEY WENT WITHOUT FEELING. "POOR DANIEL," SAID SOME PEOPLE IN THE CROWD WHO KNEW HIS NAME. "YES," SAID SOME OTHERS, "BUT AT LEAST HE HAD THAT SPECIAL HELP," THEY SAID.

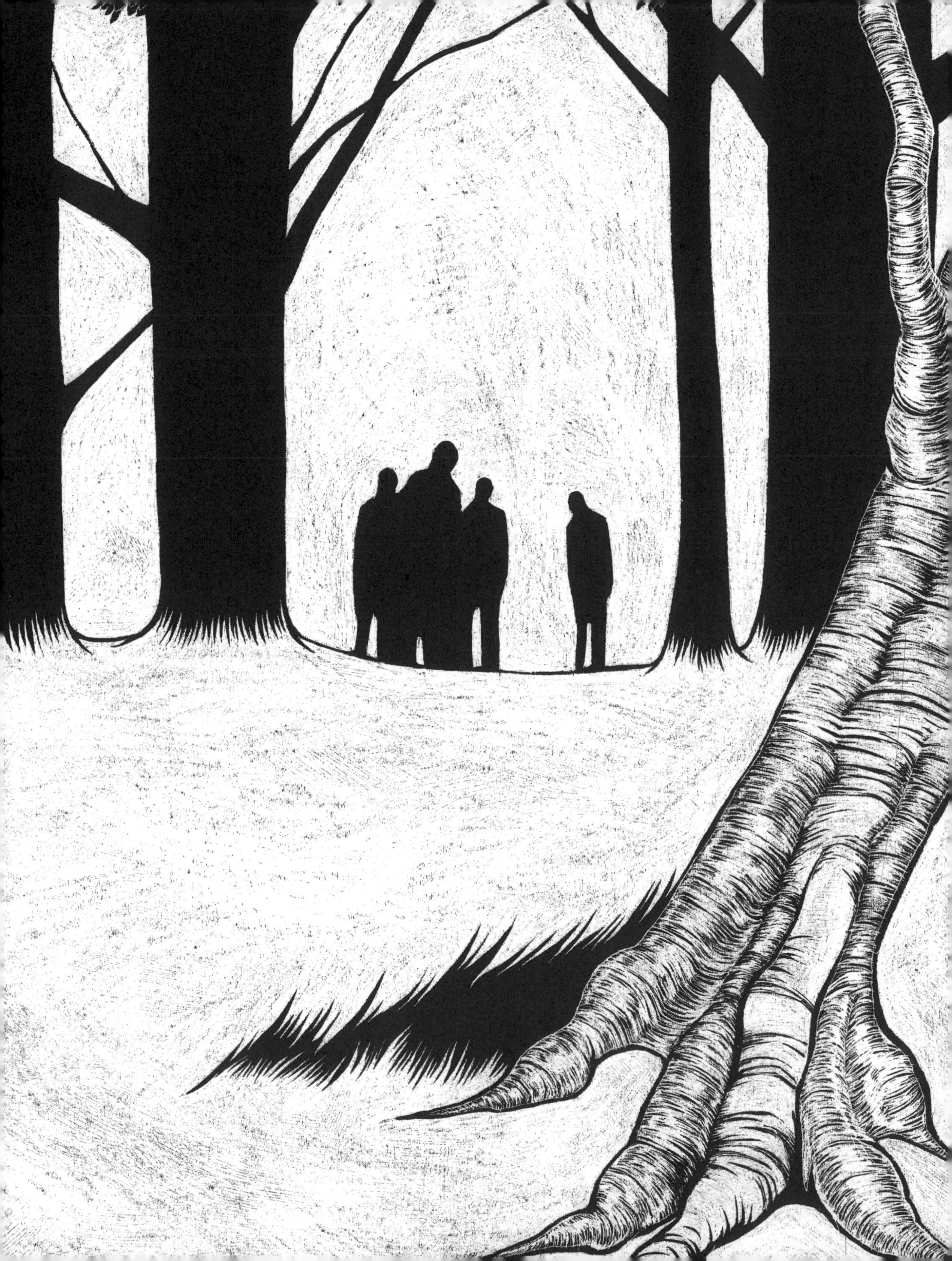

LATER, AS THE CHILDREN WALKED TOGETHER TOWARDS THEIR CAR ACROSS THE LUSH, BURIAL LANDSCAPE, THEY SAW THE WOMAN WITH THE NEEDLE. SHE WAS STANDING IN THE PARKING LOT, TAPPING HER GREEN THIGHS AND MOUTHING A CHORUS IN ANTICIPATION OF THE MOMENT WHEN THE SERVICE WAS OVER, AND SHE WOULD BE INSIDE HER CAR.

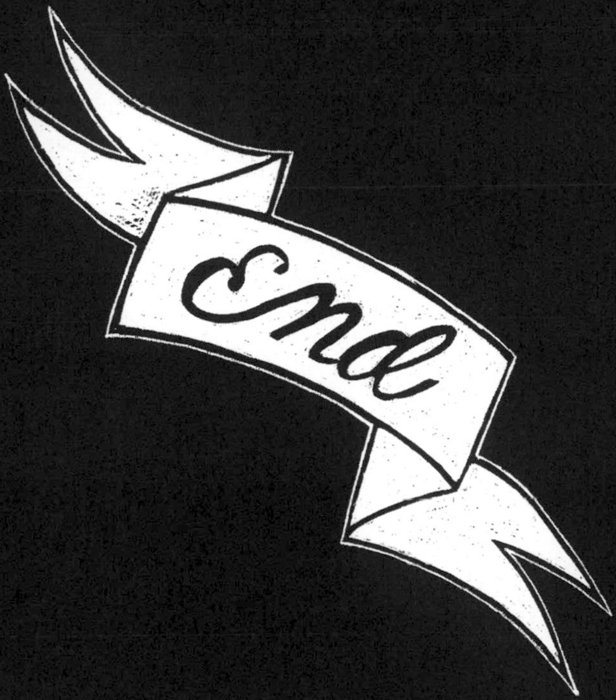
End

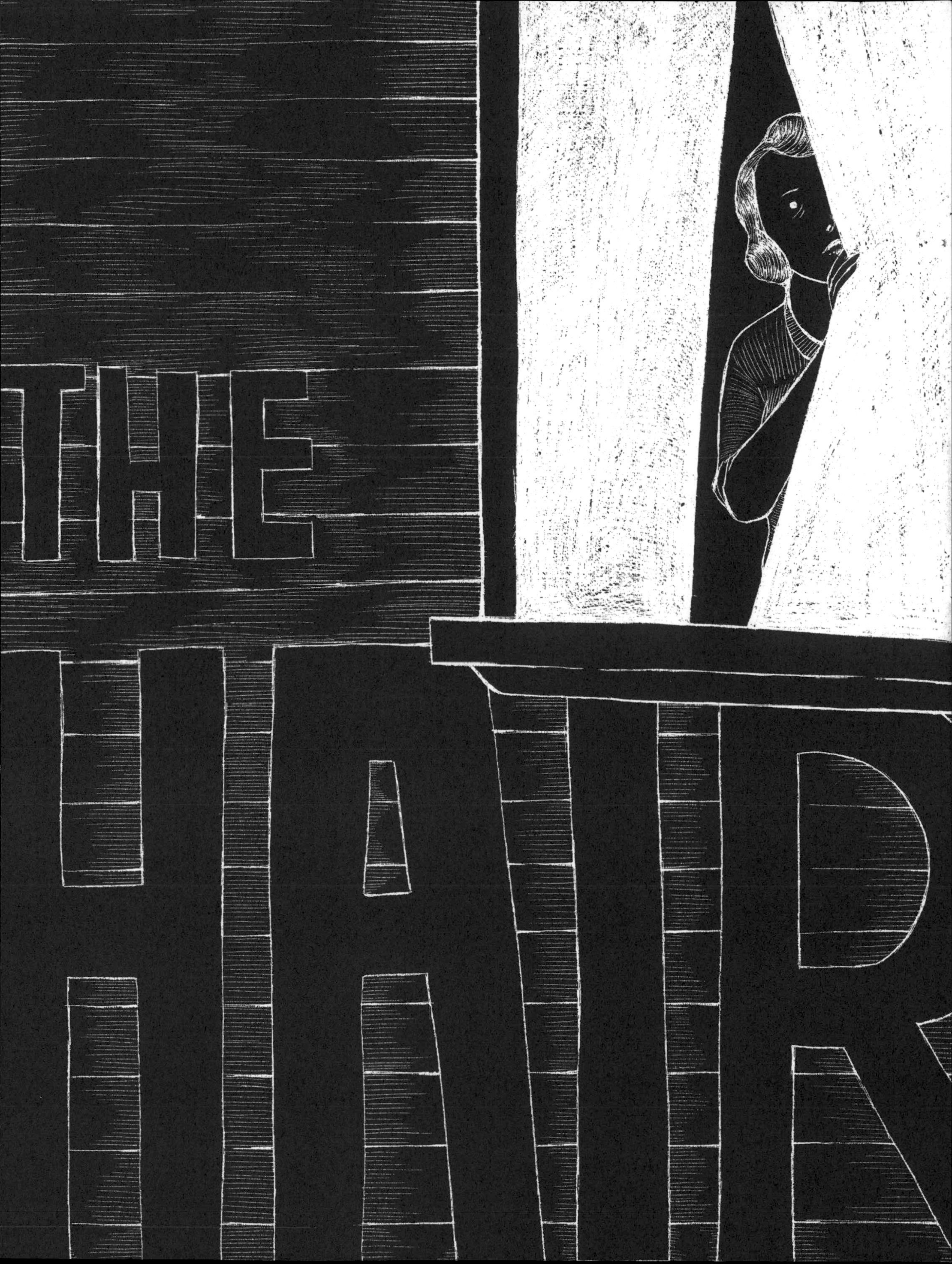
THE
HAIR

ON TUESDAY, AUGUST 21, A HOSPITAL REPORTED SEVERAL DEATHS, AND ONE UNUSUAL BIRTH.

T WAS A SLOW, HONEST HOSPITAL. WHEN PEOPLE THOUGHT OF IT, THEY
HOUGHT OF CRAWLING VINES. OTHERS THOUGHT OF COOING NURSES
ND LONG HALLS. IT WAS ON A HILL AND THE SKY WAS
RIGHT AGAINST IT DURING THE DAYTIME.

THAT DAY, A MOTHER HAD COME IN TO GIVE BIRTH. SHE WAS AT HOME BEFORE, AND HAD PRACTICED A GREAT DEAL. SHE WAS VERY BIG ALL AROUND. WHEN THEY BROUGHT HER THROUGH THE HOSPITAL DOORS, SHE NOTICED THE VINES. NURSES PUT HER IN A WHEELCHAIR AND ROLLED HER DOWN THE HALLS, HUSHING AND SIGHING. THERE WAS NO HUSBAND.

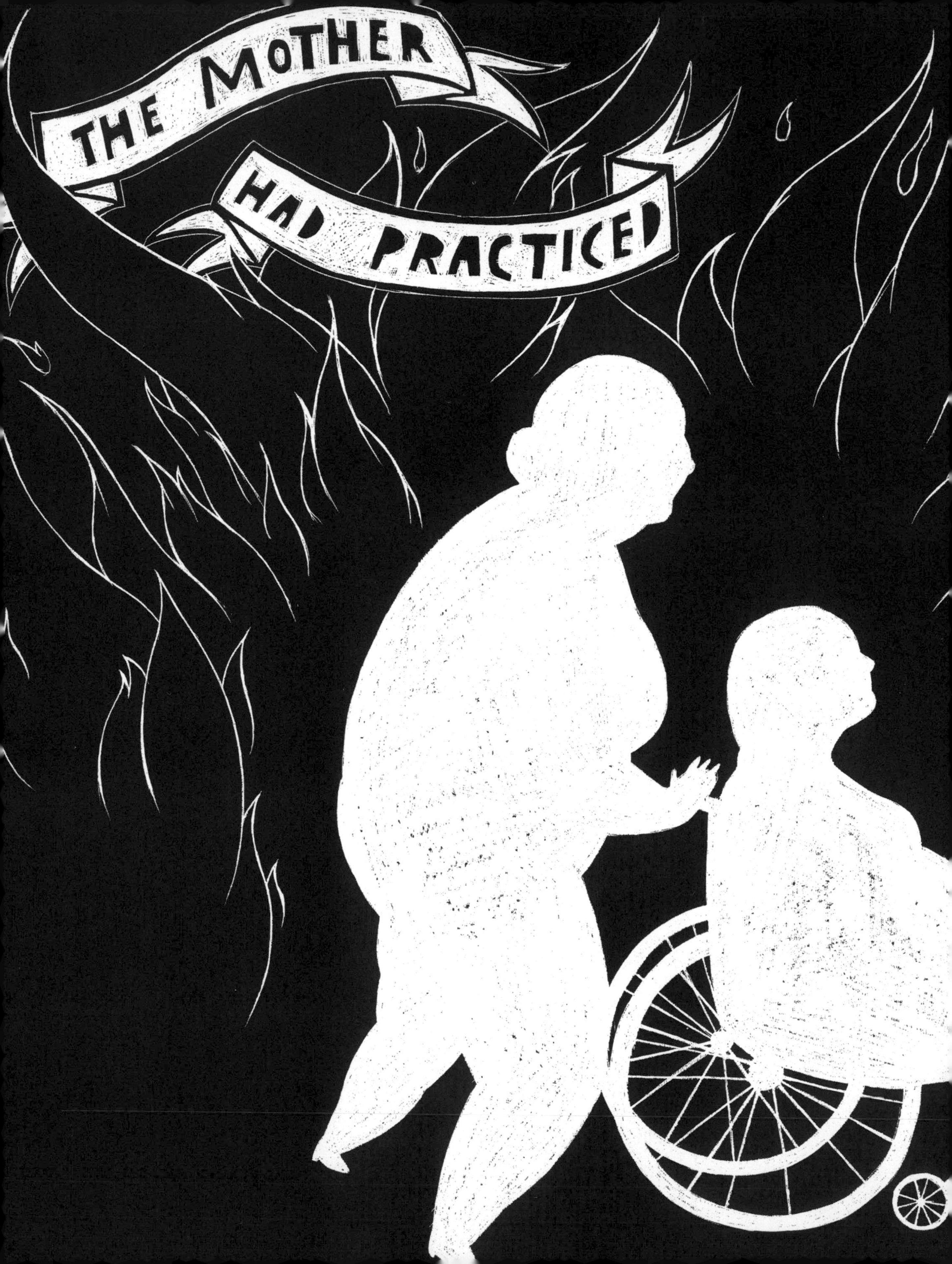
THE MOTHER
HAD PRACTICED

THE WOMAN GAVE BIRTH FOR 29 HOURS. IT WAS THE LONGEST THE HOSPITAL HAD SEEN OR WORKED ON. THEY WORKED VERY HARD HE WOMAN HAD BEEN CARRYING TWINS, AND IT WAS A SURPRISE. THE DOCTOR WAS SURPRISED, AND THE NURSES WERE AKEN ABACK. THEY HURRIED AROUND THE QUIET HALLS, BUT EPT IT TO A WHISPER.

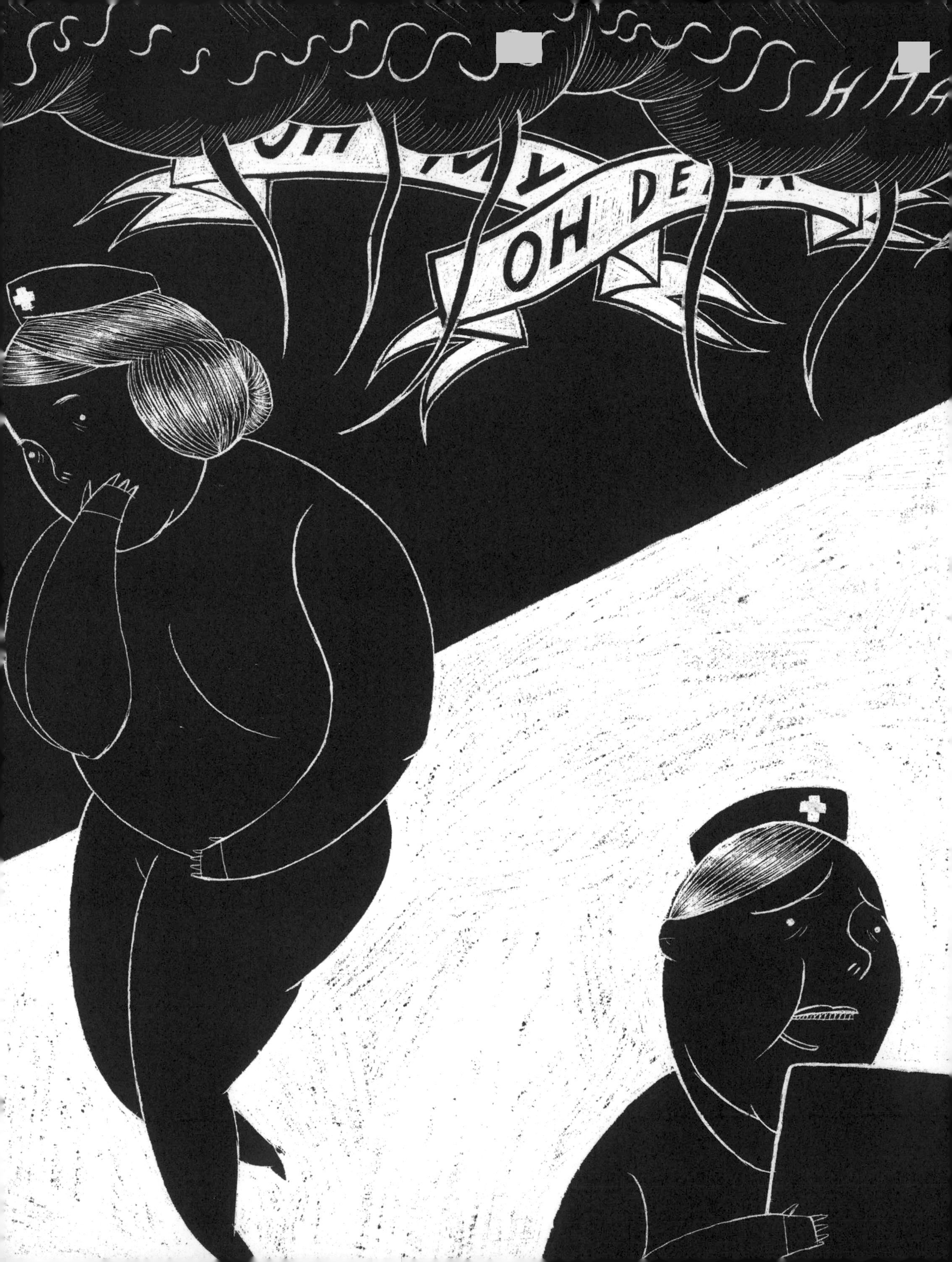
OH

SOMETHING ELSE WAS DIFFERENT, TOO. WHEN THE BABIES WERE PUSHED OUT, IT WAS CONFUSING. THE NURSES SHRIEKED WITH FEAR, THEN WONDER. THE DOCTOR COVERED HIS MOUTH. "A FIRST FOR THE HOSPITAL!" HE SAID. "OH MY," THE NURSES SAID. "WHAT IS IT?" SAID THE MOTHER.

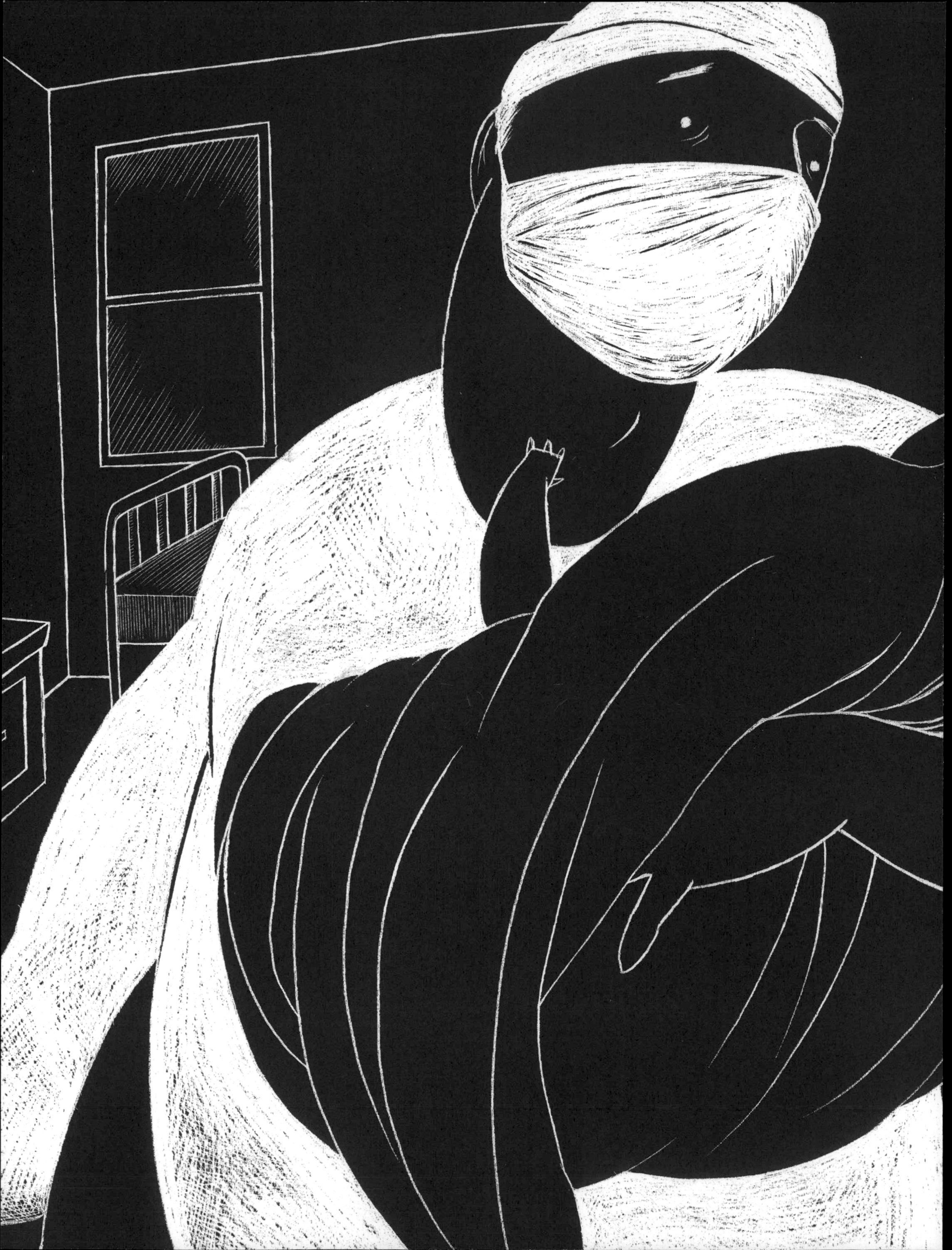

THE BABIES WERE WITH THEIR HEADS TOGETHER. IT WAS VERY SERIOUS LOOKING. THEY WERE NOT CONNECTED BY SKIN OR BONE OR MUSCLE. THEY WERE CONNECTED BY THEIR HAIR, WHICH CAME OUT IN A WISP AT THE TOP OF EACH HEAD, AND GREW GENTLY INTO EACH OTHER.
"WE SHOULD CUT IT," SAID THE NURSES, WEEPING.
"CALL THE NEWSPAPERS," SAID THE DOCTOR.

THE NURSES SHOOK THEIR HEADS AND PUT THE MOTHER IN A ROOM. "ISN'T IT HORRIBLE," THEY SAID. "I DON'T MIND, REALLY," SAID TH MOTHER, AND FELL ASLEEP.

THE NEXT WEEK, THE MOTHER STAYED IN THE HOSPITAL AND WAITED FOR THE NEWSPAPERS TO BE FINISHED. THE BABIES SLEPT TOGETHER, AND ATE AND CRIED. MANY NEWSPAPERS FROM MANY CITIES CAME FOR PICTURES AND INTERVIEWS. "HOW DOES IT FEEL TO BE THE MOTHER OF SUCH AN ASTONISHMENT?" THE NEWSPAPERS ASKED. "AT LEAST IT DOESN'T HURT THEM," SAID THE MOTHER. "HOSPITAL PERFORMS MIRACLE," SAID THE NEWSPAPERS. "SIAMESE TWINS BORN IN SMALL TOWN."
"THEY'RE NOT REALLY SIAMESE TWINS, REALLY," SAID THE MOTHER. BUT THE NEWSPAPERS DID NOT HEAR HER.

AFTER A TIME, THE REPORTERS STOPPED COMING, AND THE MOTHER WANTED TO GO HOME. "WE WILL CUT THE HAIR, NOW," SAID THE DOCTOR. "OH," SAID THE MOTHER. THE MOTHER HAD GOTTEN USE TO THE LONG STRANDS.

"MAYBE THEY ARE SUPPOSED TO BE TOGETHER," SHE SAID. "WE ARE SCIENTISTS, HERE," SAID THE DOCTOR, BOTHERED.

THE MOTHER STUFFED THINGS INTO HER SUITCASE. "LET'S LET THEM DECIDE FOR THEMSELVES WHEN THEY ARE BIGGER," SHE SAID. "LOOK," SAID THE DOCTOR. "IT WILL NOT HURT THEM. IT'S JUST HAIR." THE MOTHER WAS LOOKING AT THE LINOLEUM. AFTER A WHILE THEY GAVE HER A SANDWICH AND LET HER GO HOME.

THE MOTHER DID NOT CUT THEIR HAIR.

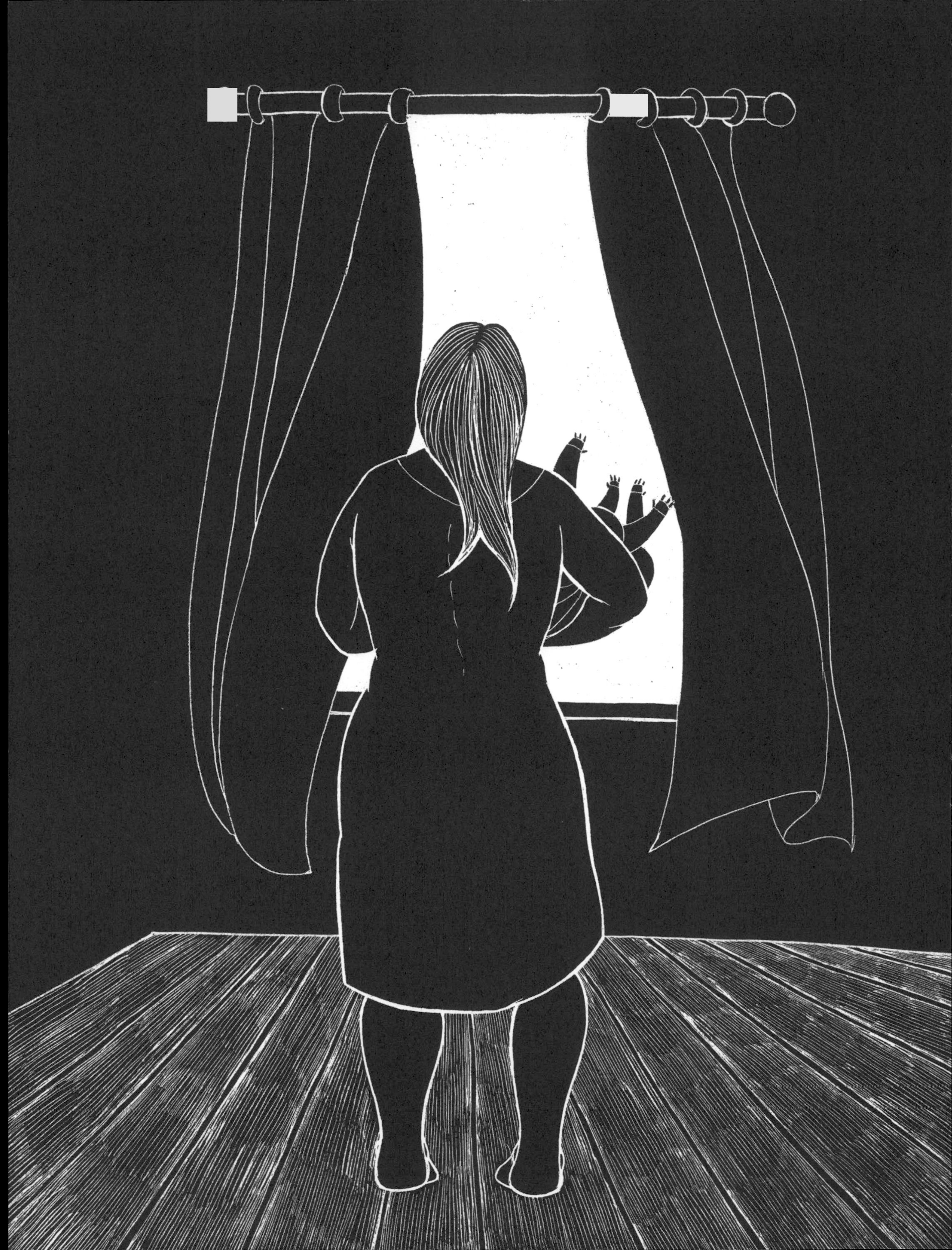

THE BABIES WERE GIRLS, AND TURNED OUT TO BE VERY GOOD AND STRONG. AFTER A SHORT WHILE, THE MOTHER DID NOT EVEN NOTICE THAT THEY WERE CONNECTED. SHE FED THEM AND BATHED THEM AND HELD THEM WITH BOTH ARMS. THEIR HAIR BEGAN TO GROW, AND THEY COULD MOVE APART BIT BY BIT. WHEN THE MOTHER TOOK THEM OUTSIDE OF THE HOUSE, PEOPLE ON THE STREET RECOGNIZED THE FAMILY FROM THE NEWSPAPERS. THEY BECAME VERY FAMOUS. THE HOSPITAL ALSO BECAME VERY FAMOUS, AND WAS KNOWN FOR ITS GENTLENESS AND UNDERSTANDING. MANY NEIGHBORS GAVE ADVICE TO THE MOTHER ABOUT WHAT TO DO. "CUT IT OFF," SAID SOME PEOPLE. "THEY WILL DIE IF YOU CUT IT," SAID OTHER PEOPLE. "IT'S WHAT MAKES THEM SPECIAL," SAID THE MOTHER.

VERY SLOWLY, THE BABIES BEGAN TO NOTICE EACH OTHER. THEY LAUGHED AND LAUGHED. THE MOTHER COULD LEAVE THEM ALONE ON THE LIVING ROOM FLOOR FOR HOURS. THEY WOULD ROLL AROUND AND SPEAK TO EACH OTHER IN LANGUAGES SHE COULD NOT UNDERSTAND. ONE THING THAT WAS INTERESTING WAS THAT THEY NEVER PULLED AWAY FROM EACH OTHER. IF THEY ROLLED TOO FAR, THEY WOULD ROLL BACK BEFORE THE HAIR BEGAN TO TUG AT THEIR SCALPS.

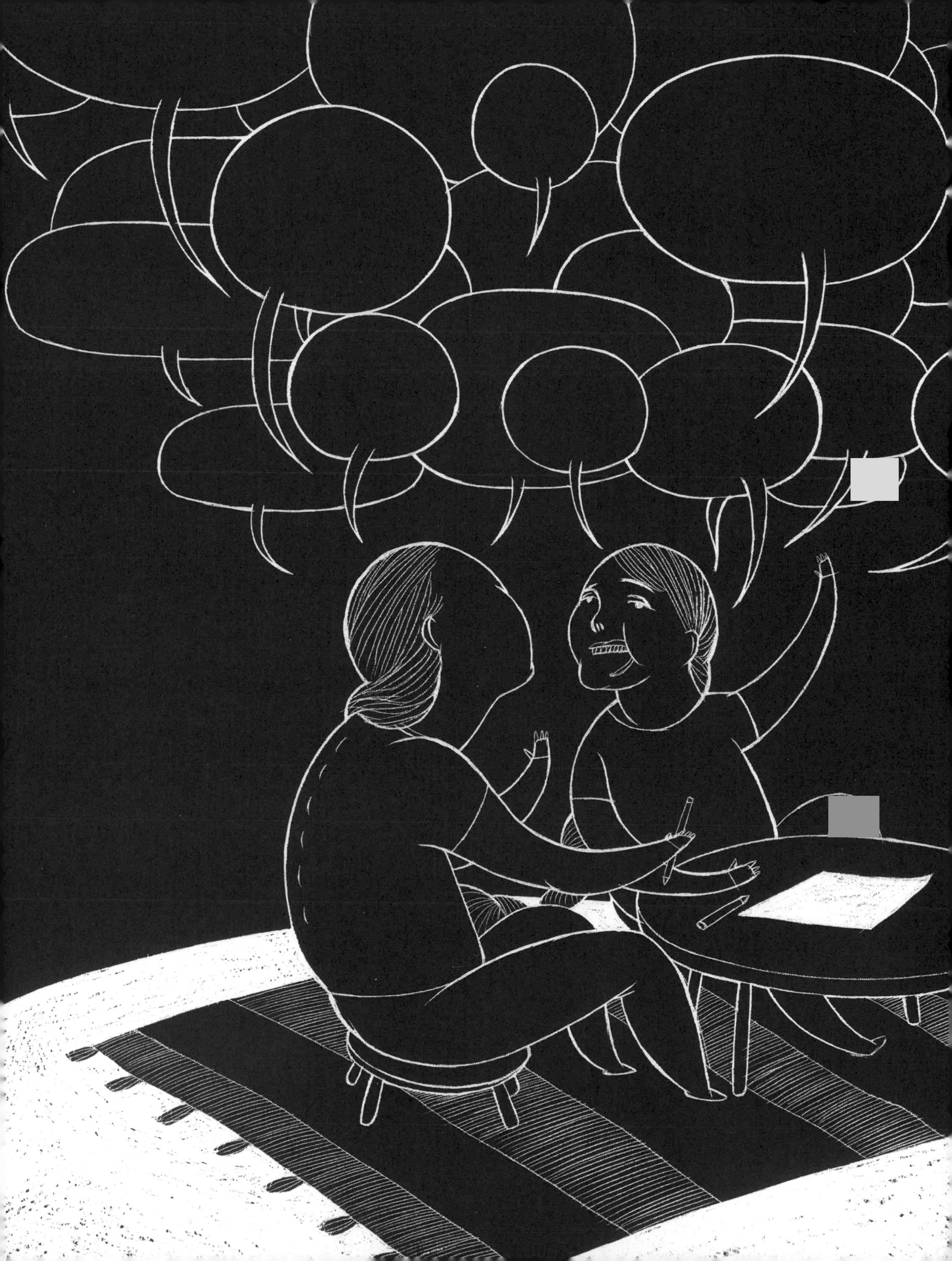

WHEN THEY GREW UP ENOUGH TO STAND, THE HAIR HAD GROWN SO LONG THAT THEY COULD WALK THREE FEET AWAY FROM EACH OTHER IN ALL DIRECTIONS. THEN IT STOPPED. THE MOTHER WAS WORRIED THAT IT WOULD GROW AND GROW FOREVER, UNTIL THE GIRLS WERE SO FAR APART THAT THEY WOULD HAVE TO STAND IN SEPERATE ROOMS. BUT IT DID NOT; AFTER EXACTLY THREE FEET, IT STOPPED FOR GOOD. THE MOTHER WOULD BRAID IT SO THAT IT HUNG DOWN THEIR BACKS AND BACK UP INTO THEIR HEADS AGAIN, LIKE A ROPE. IT WAS HEAVY AND SLIPPERY. THEY SAT ACROSS FROM EACH OTHER IN THE DINING ROOM, DRAWING PICTURES AND SMILING, THEIR BRAID WHAPPING THE LEGS OF THE TABLE. SOMETIMES THE GIRLS ASKED THEIR MOTHER WHY OTHER PEOPLE WEREN'T CONNECTED BY HAIR. "YOU ARE SPECIAL," SHE SAID. "EVERYONE ELSE IS AWAY FROM EACH OTHER ALL THE TIME."

WHEN THE GIRLS WERE 9, A NEW DOCTOR VISITED THEM AT HOME. THEY WERE DRAWING WITH COLORED CHALK. HE SPOKE TO THE MOTHER IN THE LIVING ROOM FOR A LONG TIME. WHEN THEY CAME OUT, THE DOCTOR LOOKED AT THE GIRLS AND TOUCHED THE THICK BRAID. "YOU COULD ALWAYS SAVE IT IN A DRAWER," HE SAID, LEAVING. THE MOTHER'S EYES WERE RED FROM CRYING.

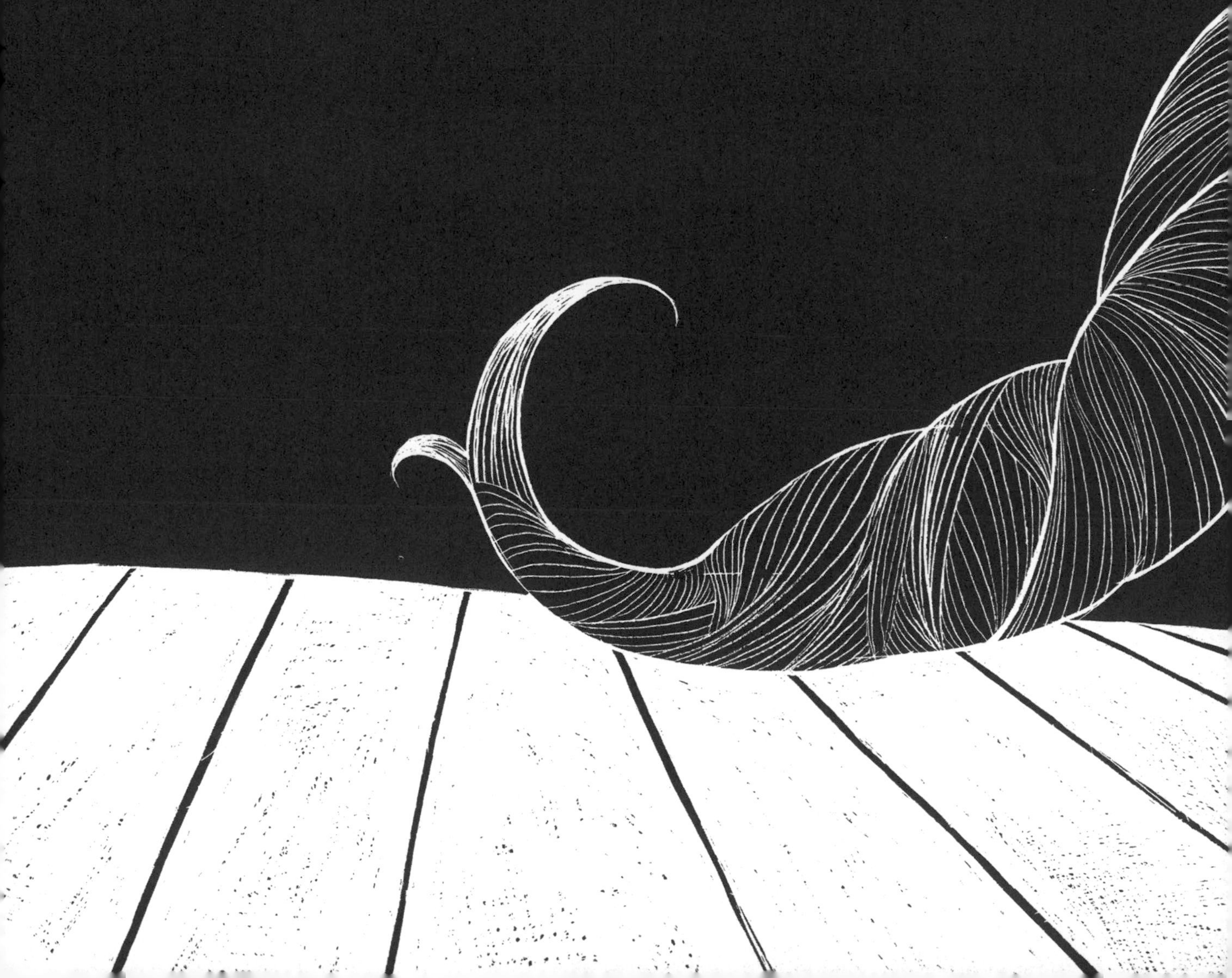

THAT NIGHT, SHE WENT TO THE GIRLS IN THEIR ROOM.
SHE SAT ON THE DOUBLE BED WITH YELLOW COVERS. SHE
TOLD THEM ABOUT HOW THEY COULD BE SEPARATE PEOPLE.
THAT THEY COULD WALK ANYWHERE THEY WANTED, ALONE
IF THEY WANTED. "YOU COULD EVEN LIVE IN SEPARATE
CITIES," SHE SAID, WEEPING. THE GIRLS HAD NEVER
THOUGHT OF THIS BEFORE. THEY CRINGED, AND FOR
THE FIRST TIME EVER, HAD THE OPPOSITE THOUGHT AT
THE SAME TIME.

THE MOTHER STOOD THEM IN FRONT OF THE MIRROR AND
DRESSED THEM IN DIFFERENT CLOTHES. SHE HELD BACK
THEIR HAIR. THE GIRLS LOOKED AT THEMSELVES. "IT'S
TERRIBLE," SAID ONE GIRL. THE OTHER GIRL WAS QUIET.
"YOU DECIDE," SAID THE MOTHER. THEY WENT TO BED,
AND DID NOT WHISPER ALL NIGHT.
THE MOTHER ALSO WENT TO BED, SIGHING WITH
SADNESS AND HOPE.

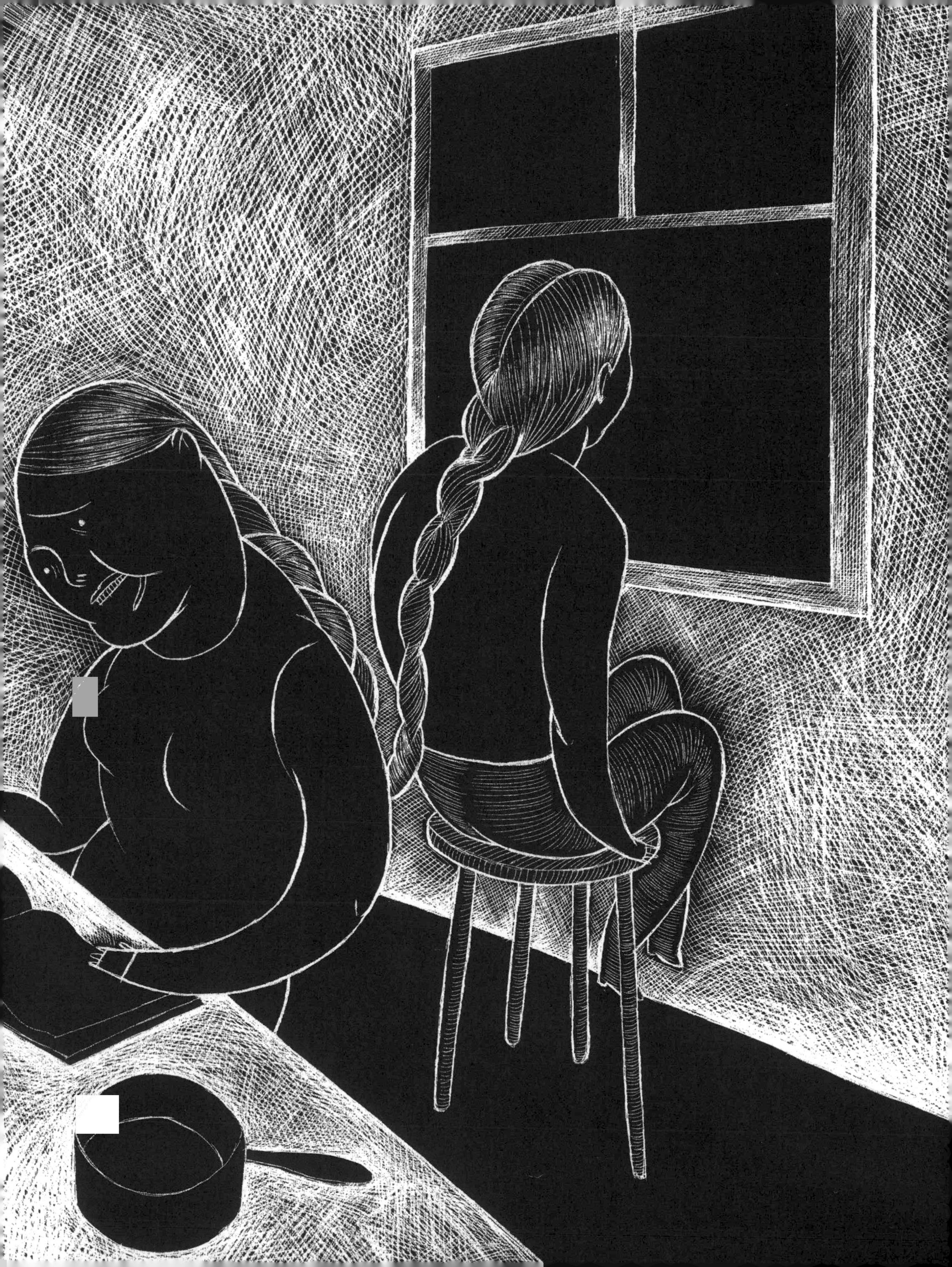

FOR A LONG TIME, THE GIRLS DID NOTHING. IT HAD BECOME CLEAR. ONE GIRL TRIED TO PLAY GAMES WITH HER SISTER AND TELL HER JOKES. SHE BRAIDED THE HAIR AND COMBED IT AND REMINDED HER SISTER OF HOW BEAUTIFUL IT WAS. SHE COOKED HER SISTER MEALS. THE OTHER GIRL BECAME SILENT ALL THE TIME, AND STARED OUT WINDOW THEY STARTED TO ARGUE. EACH GIRL THOUGHT THAT SHE COULD CONVINCE THE OTHER.

THE ONE SISTER BEGAN TO PLOT HOW SHE COULD CUT THE HAIR IN THE NIGHT. SHE FELT A GREAT GUILT. ONE NIGHT SHE STOLE SCISSORS FROM THE KITCHEN AND BROUGHT THEM TO BED WITH HER. SHE LAY AWAKE IN THE DARK, PANTING. IN THE MORNING SHE RETURNED THEM, UNUSED, AND WAITED UNTIL THE NEXT NIGHT. NIGHT AFTER NIGHT SHE HELD THE SCISSORS. THE MOTHER LET THIS GO ON FOR MANY YEARS.

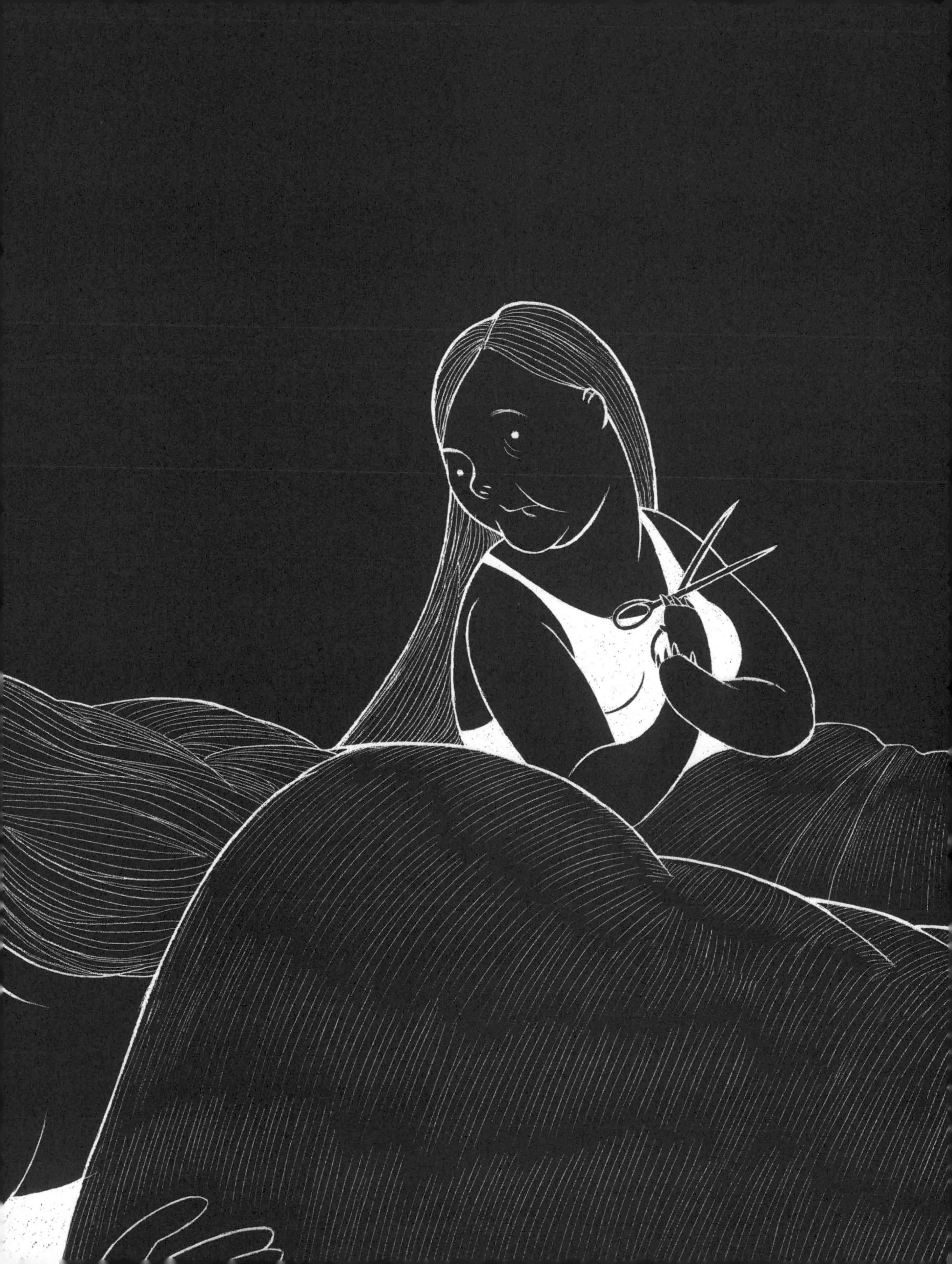

WHEN SHE TURNED 16, THE SISTER THAT DID NOT WANT TO SEPARATE MADE THE OTHER ONE A MAP OF SOME COUNTRY. "WE HAVE NOT BEEN HERE," SHE SAID, POINTING TO JAPAN. THE OTHER SISTER DID NOT SAY ANYTHING. THE NEXT MORNING SHE WAS GONE.

THE OTHER SISTER DID NOT NOTICE UNTIL SHE OPENED HER EYES. SHE RAN TO THE MIRROR TO SEE IF IT WAS TRUE. HER MOTHER FOUND HER ON THE BATHROOM FLOOR, WEEPING. SHE LAY DOWN NEXT TO HER AND THEY DID NOT GET UP FOR MANY HOURS.

AFTER A LONG TIME, THE SISTER GOT UP AND LEFT THE HOUSE. HER SHORT HAIR JERKED AROUND HER SHOULDERS, UNEVEN. SHE SEARCHED THROUGH THE NEIGHBORS YARDS, THE PARK, THE HIGH SCHOOL, THE GYM. SHE LOOKED AND CALLED OUT HER SISTER'S NAME. SHE LOOKED FOR SEVERAL YEARS.

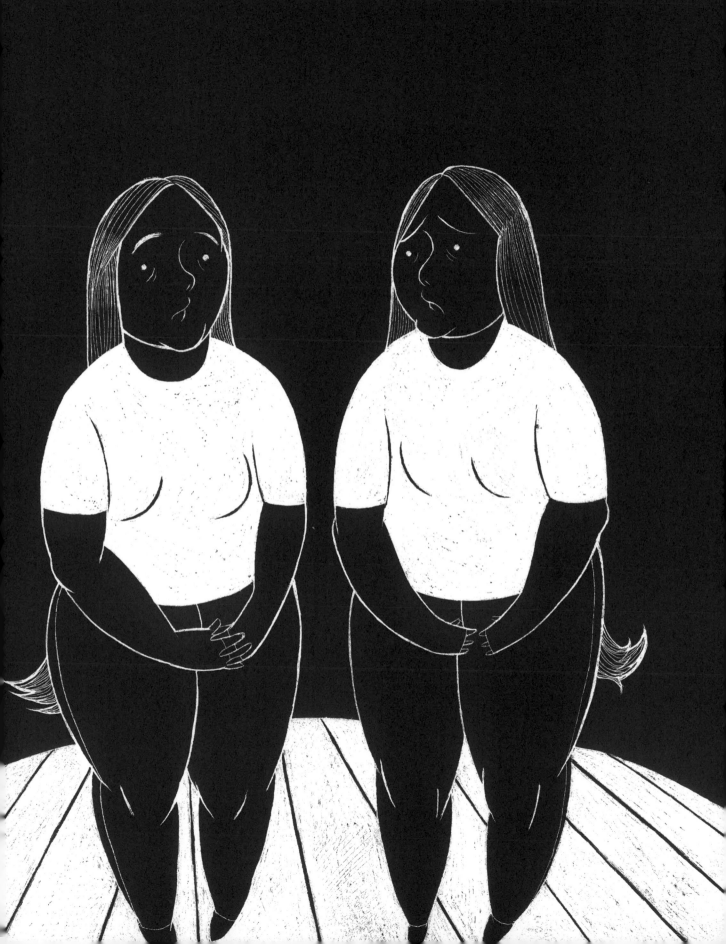

WHEN SHE WAS OLD ENOUGH TO MOVE OUT OF HER MOTHER'S HOUSE, THE SISTER PICKED A CITY FAR AWAY TO LIVE IN. HER MOTHER DROVE HER THERE IN THE CAR. AS THEY DROVE FARTHER AND FARTHER AWAY, THE SISTER LOOKED OUT THE WINDOW AND LET HER HEAD BUMP AGAINST THE GLASS. SHE SAW FOLIAGE ALONG THE SIDE OF THE ROAD THAT SHE DID NOT RECOGNIZE, AND SHE KNEW HER LIFE WAS GOING TO BE EXCITING.

THE SISTER LIKED HER NEW APARTMENT. SHE LET HER HAIR GROW TO A LENGTH, AND BRAIDED IT EVERYDAY AS IF IT WERE CONNECTED TO SOMETHING. SHE HAD A BATHROOM AND A BEDROOM AND A WINDOW. EVERY MONTH SHE GOT A HAIRCUT, AND AFTERWARDS SHE WOULD BE SICK. ONE MORNING SHE NOTICED THAT ONE STRAND OF HAIR SEEMED TO BE LONGER THAN THE OTHERS. SHE CUT IT OFF IN THE MIRROR. "HMMM," SHE SAID.

A COUPLE OF DAYS LATER, IT WAS AGAIN LONGER THAN THE REST. "HOW FUNNY," SHE THOUGHT. SHE CUT IT OFF RIGHT AWAY, AND WENT OUTSIDE. THE MAN AT THE GROCERY STORE POINTED AT HER NECK. "I THINK YOUR BARBER FORGOT SOMETHING," HE SAID. THE HAIR WAS CLIMBING DOWN HER FRONT. THE SISTER TURNED VERY PALE AND RAN HOME. BY THE TIME SHE HAD SHUT THE DOOR BEHIND HER, IT WAS DOWN TO HER KNEES.

SHE STAYED AWAKE MOST OF THE NIGHT WATCHING, BUT IT SEEMED TO STOP, SO SHE WENT TO SLEEP.

THE NEXT MORNING IT WAS DOWN TO HER ANKLES. SHE
DID NOT LEAVE THE HOUSE. BY THE MIDDLE OF THE DAY
THE OTHER HAIRS HAD BEGUN TO GROW AS WELL. SOME
WERE DOWN TO HER FEET, AND SHE PILED THEM UP IN
A WISP NEXT TO HER CHAIR. SHE READ A BOOK CALLED,
"A HISTORY OF EMPTINESS," AND WAITED. SHE WAS
VERY SCARED AND TIRED AT THE SAME TIME. AFTER A
WHILE SHE DOZED OFF, AND WHEN SHE WOKE, THE
ENDS OF HER HAIR WERE NOWHERE TO BE SEEN.

THE STRANDS WERE THIN AND LIGHT, AND THE SISTER
FOLLOWED THEM ALONG THE FLOORBOARDS AND UNDER
THE DOOR. SHE OPENED THE DOOR AND FOLLOWED THE
HAIR DOWN THE STAIRS. HER HEART WAS BEATING
VERY FAST. SHE FOLLOWED THE STRANDS OUT OF THE
BUILDING, AND THEY MADE SHINY LINES ALONG THE
SIDEWALK. THERE WERE PEOPLE ON THE STREET, AND
THEY WATCHED HER HUNCHED OVER THE STREET,
LOOKING.

THE SISTER FOLLOWED THE HAIR ALONG MANY BLOCKS, ALL OVER THE CITY. IT CURLED AROUND LAMPOSTS AND SLUNK ACROSS COBBLESTONE.
SHE SAW IT CURL AROUND A FINAL BEND BEFORE IT DISSAPEARED UNDER THE FRONT DOOR OF A BUILDING. IN A WINDOW FAR ABOVE, A WOMAN PULLED BACK THE BLINDS AND LOOKED DOWN ONTO THE STREET AT THE GIRL. THE WOMAN CRIED WITH JOY. WHEN THE SISTER OPENED THE DOOR TO THE BUILDING, SHE SAW THE END OF HER HAIR AS IT CRAWLED SLOWLY UP THE STAIRS. SHE NOTICED OTHER HAIR, COMING FROM THE OPPOSITE DIRECTION. IT SPILLED DOWN FROM THE TOP OF THE STAIRS. THE HALLWAY WAS A SEA OF STRANDS. THE SISTER STEPPED OVER MOUNDS UNTIL SHE WAS AT A DOOR. IT WAS A NORMAL DOOR, WITH HAIR COMING OUT FROM UNDER IT, LIKE A STREAM.

THE DOOR OPENED AND THE TWO SISTERS LOOKED AT EACH OTHER. THEIR FACES WERE FULL GROWN AND DIM. EVERYWHERE THERE WAS HAIR - IT BUNCHED AROUND THEIR ANKLES AND THEY SWOOPED DOWN TO PICK IT UP WITH THEIR HANDS. WHEN THEY GOT INSIDE THE SMALL APARTMENT, HAIR CLUMPED AND CLIMBED AROUND THE WALLS. THE ROOM WAS A DOWNY, BROWN EXPANSE.
"I FORGIVE YOU," SAID ONE SISTER, FINALLY. "ME TOO," SAID THE OTHER. AFTER THAT THEY DID NOT SAY ANYTHING MORE ABOUT IT EVER AGAIN.

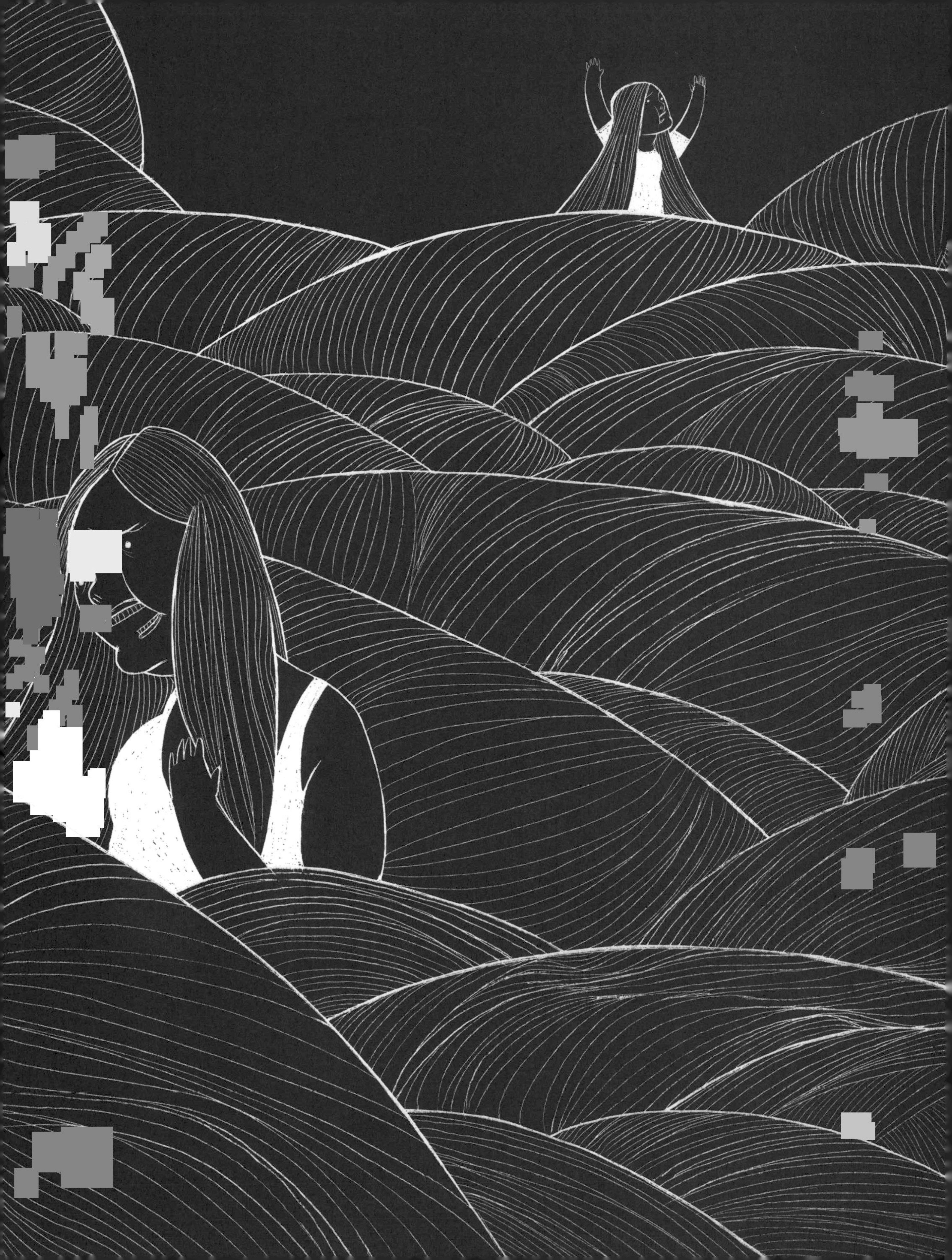

AFTER THEY HAD FINISHED MOVING IN TOGETHER, THE SISTERS'S HAIR GREW BACK UNTIL IT WAS ONE HEAVY BRAID AGAIN. IT SHORTENED SLOWLY OVER TIME, UNTIL THEY COULD WALK THREE FEET APART IN ALL DIRECTIONS, AND THEN IT STOPPED. EVERY DAY THEY COOKED EACH OTHER MEALS AND LOOKED OUT THE WINDOW, SIDE BY SIDE. YEARS LATER, AFTER THEY HAD DIED, THE APARTMENT WAS RENTED OUT TO A FAMILY WITH LITTLE CHILDREN WHO FOUND SPACES IN THE WALL WITH HOLES IN IT WHERE THE SISTERS KEPT DRAWINGS THEY HAD DONE. ALL OF THE DRAWINGS LOOKED THE SAME AND WERE OF ONE PERSON ALONE IN A ROOM.

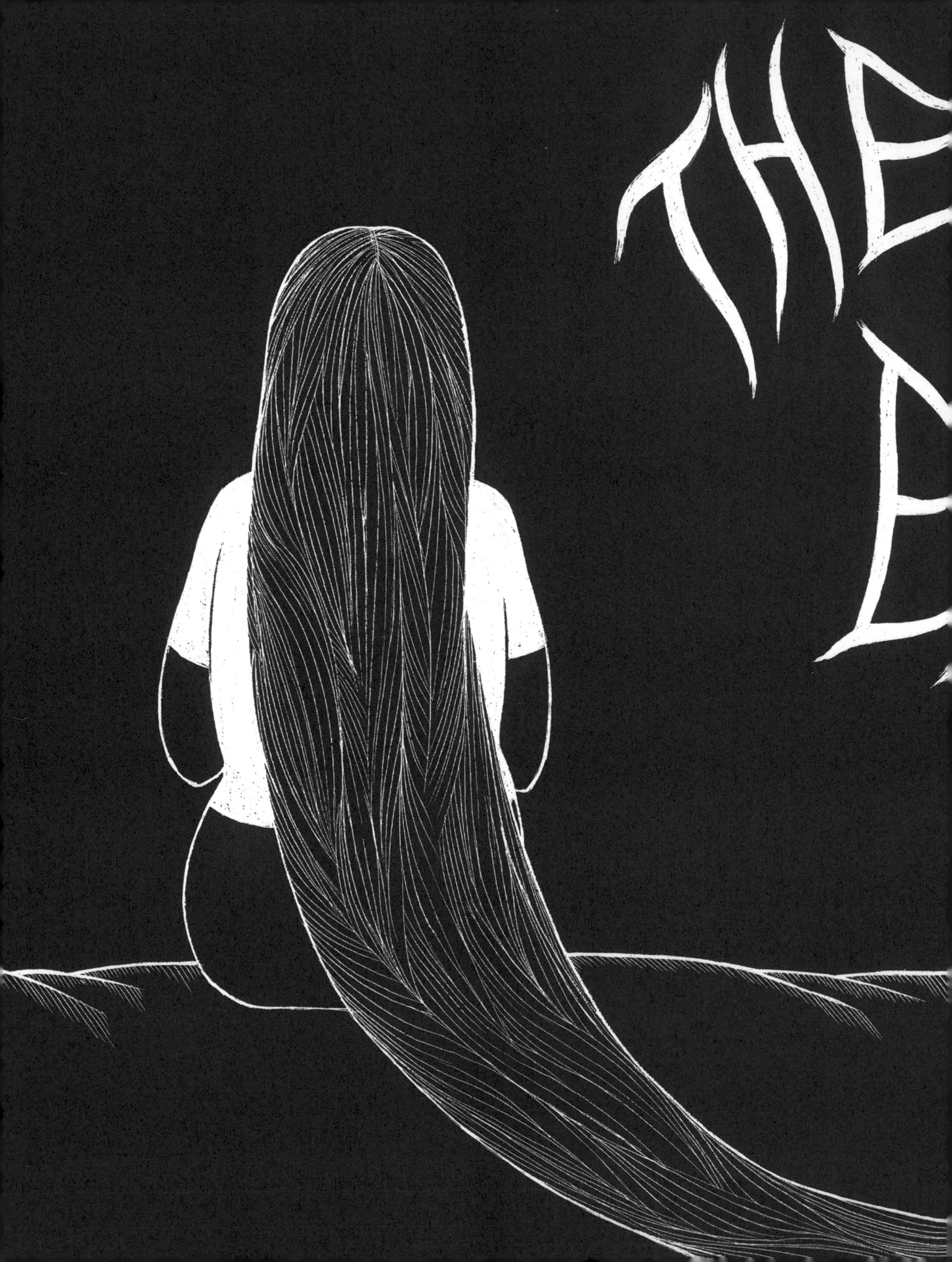
THE

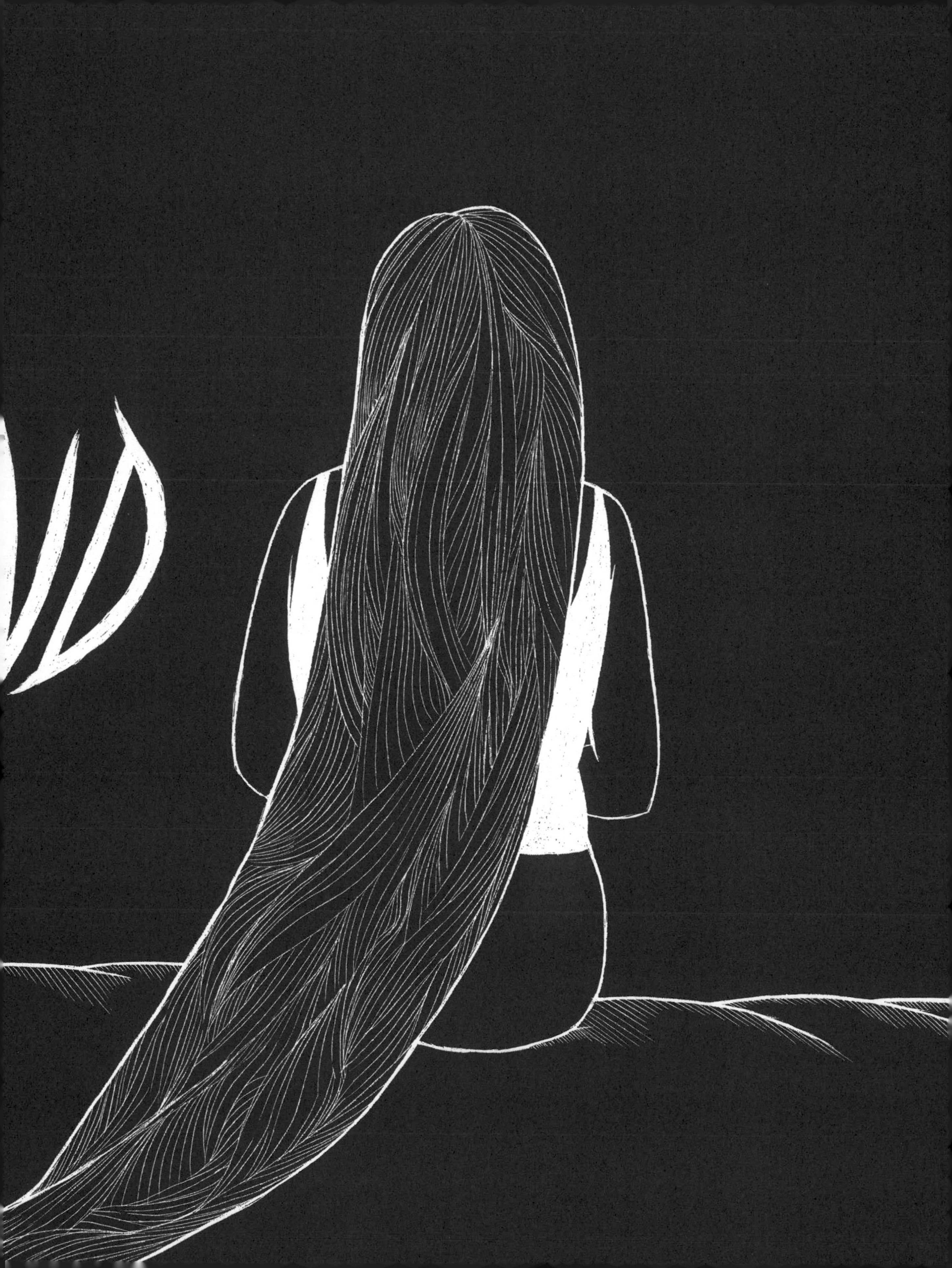